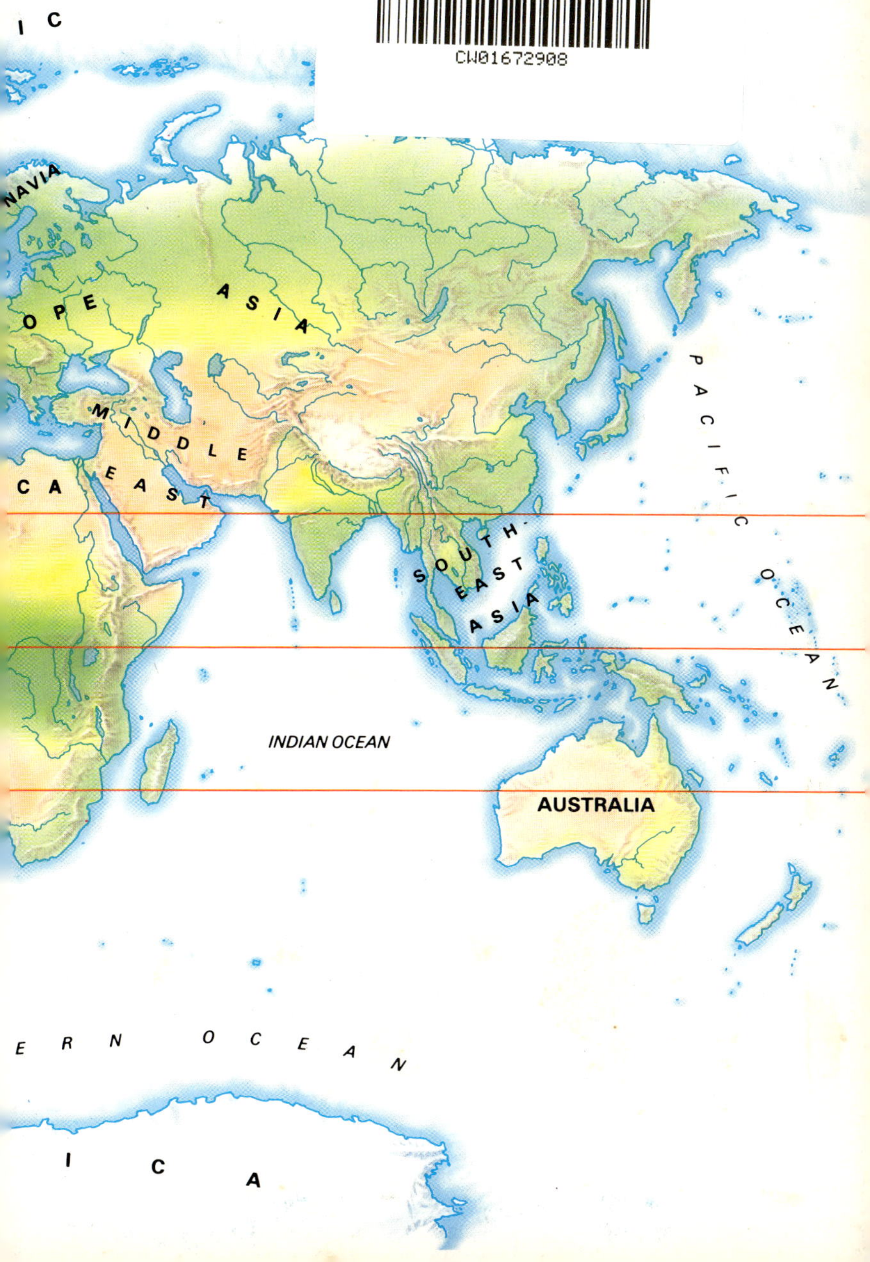
I C
NAVIA
OPE
ASIA
MIDDLE EAST
CA
PACIFIC OCEAN
SOUTH-EAST ASIA
INDIAN OCEAN
AUSTRALIA
ERN OCEAN
I C A

To Rachel and Steven

First published in 1983 by
Kingfisher Books Limited
Elsley Court, 20–22 Great
Titchfield Street, London W1P 7AD

BRITISH LIBRARY CATALOGUING
IN PUBLICATION DATA
Wright, David and Jill
Pocket atlas. – (Kingfisher pocket books)
1. Atlases
I. Title
912 G1021
ISBN 0 86272 053 2

Design by John Strange
Cover design by Pinpoint Design Company
Illustrations by Mike Saunders and David Wright
Maps by Product (Graphics) Support Limited and Malcolm Porter
Printed in Italy by Vallardi Industrie Grafiche, Milan
Phototypeset by Southern Positives & Negatives (SPAN), Lingfield, Surrey

Photographs; A.N.I.B. 171 *bottom*; J. Allan Cash Photo Library 14, 30, 45, 60, 66 *left*, 79 *right*, 96, 129, 139, 161, 180, 181; Dave Collins 97, 104; Alan Hutchinson 110; Japan Information Service 84–85; High Commissioner for New Zealand 165; Royal Netherlands Embassy 37; Novosti 70, 71; Ordnance Survey 23; G.R. Roberts 31, 162, 164; Thailand Tourist Board 75; U.N.I.C.E.F. 19; Jill and David Wright 8, 26, 34, 44, 47, 54, 55, 66–67, 105, 113, 133, 136, 177, 178, 179, 181; Louise Wright 159; Z.E.F.A. 15, 40, 50, 62, 72, 79 *left*, 95, 117, 125, 132, 134, 142, 143, 147, 152, 154–155, 169, 170, 171 *top*, 172.

Picture Research: Jackie Cookson

KINGFISHER
POCKET
ATLAS

Jill and David Wright

Kingfisher Books

Contents

▶ **Flooded rice fields** on the island of Bali, Indonesia (in South-East Asia).

Introduction

This atlas is designed as an easy-to-use reference book. It is divided into sections, each of which has a colour code. For instance, the section on Europe begins with a blue stripe and the pages that follow on European countries are all marked with a blue 'thumbprint'.

Size, population, main exports and other useful information are summarized on charts. Often it is difficult to give exact figures. Even the size of a country may not always be accurately measured when there are unexplored jungles and precipitous mountains. Population figures are obtained from census records – but imagine the difficulties of counting people in a large country where travel is difficult and many people cannot read or write. There can be problems too in deciding where a river begins and ends or the precise edge of a city. This is why statistics in books do not always agree.

Products that are exported can be measured by weight or by value: diamonds may be at the top of the list in value, but at the bottom in weight! And countries can earn money in ways that are difficult to measure: by catering for tourists, or running banks, or using their ships or ports to take imports and exports for other countries.

If you are puzzled by any of the geographical words written in *italics*, each is explained in the glossary on page 176. The map index on page 182 will help you find where places are in the atlas.

Using Maps

Maps are the most important part of an atlas. They are drawn to show the surface of the Earth. **Distance** can be worked out by using the scale line. If you put a strip of paper next to the scale line of each map and mark off the kilometres shown, you can make your own 'scale ruler' to move over the map and measure distances. On the maps and in the fact boxes abbreviations are used for distance – km for kilometres and m for metres. **Direction** is shown by the compass arrow. For almost all maps, north is at the top of the page. **Height** is always difficult to show on a flat map. The main mountain ranges are shaded. The range of shading and the other symbols are shown on the key opposite, which you should use with all the maps in this atlas. **Vegetation** types are shown in different colours below. In some parts of the world the natural vegetation has long been replaced by farmland.

Main rivers and lakes are marked, but there is not enough room for every one. A 'small-scale' map of a number of large countries will have less space for detail than a 'large-scale' map of a small country. Similarly only important towns can be shown. The capital city (which is not always the largest) has a special symbol. National boundaries are marked by red lines.

▼ **The border** between Ghana and Upper Volta, in West Africa.

KEY TO VEGETATION

Moun-tains	Plains	
		Tundra (cold, treeless)
		Forest (hot or cold)
		Grassland (hot or cold)
		Dry grassland or semi-desert (very low rainfall)
		Desert

Kilometres
0 200 400 600 800
0 250 500
Miles

Scale

▲
N

NATURAL FEATURES
(*italic* letters)

River
eg Lualaba

Lake
eg Lake Victoria

Mountain peak *eg Mt Kilimanjaro*

Mountain range

Location map

▲ **Use the location maps** to find where a particular country or region is in the world.

MAN-MADE FEATURES
(non-italic letters)

ZAIRE — **Name of country in CAPITAL LETTERS**

■ **Nairobi** — **Capital City**

● Mombasa — **Other city or large town**

Boundary

The World

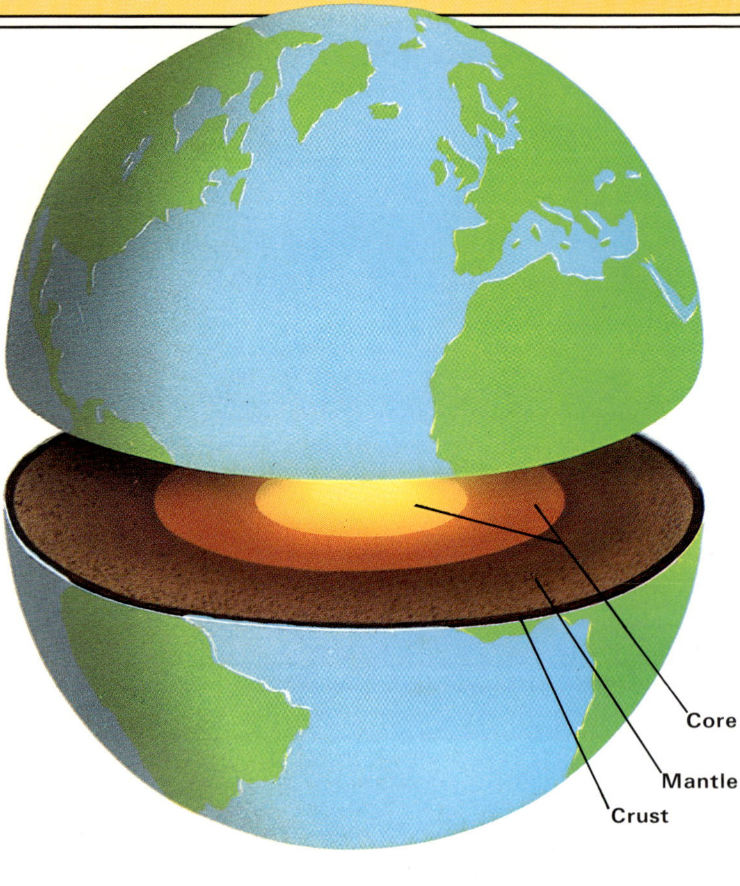

The first man on the Moon said that the Earth "looks like a beautiful jewel in space". The colours of the continents, the blue oceans, and the swirls of cloud in the *atmosphere* make fascinating patterns.

The Earth is one of nine planets which spin round the Sun. Because the Earth is neither too hot nor too cold, and because it has water and an atmosphere composed of life-supporting gases, life as we know it can exist.

Geologists and geophysicists, the people who study the Earth, believe that it is made of several layers. The crust or outer layer is comparatively thin. It is thicker beneath the continents, which are

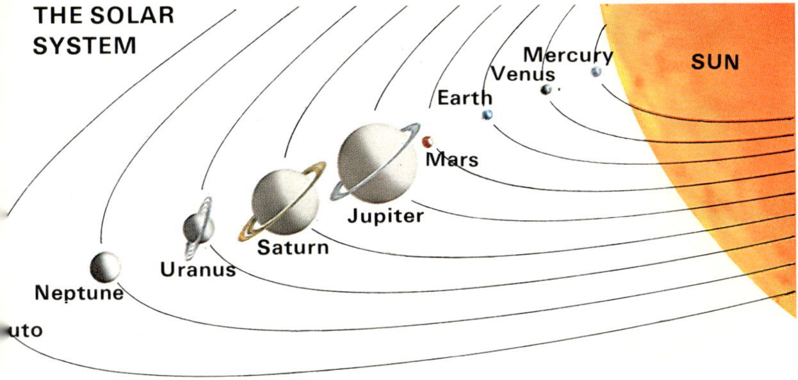

EARTH FACTS

Circumference round the Equator: 40,075 km.
Circumference round the Poles: 40,007 km.
Distance to centre of Earth: about 6370 km.
Surface area: about 510,065,600 sq km; sea covers 71% of the surface of the Earth.
Average distance from the Sun: 149,600,000 km; the Earth is further away from the Sun in July than in January.
Rotation Speed: at the Equator, the Earth rotates on its axis at 1660 km per hour.
Speed in orbit: The Earth travels at 29·8 km per second.
Average distance from Moon: 385,000 km.
Chief gases of the atmosphere: nitrogen (78%), oxygen (21%).
Chief elements of the Earth's crust: oxygen (46·6%), silicon (27·7%), aluminium (8·1%), iron (5%).

made of lighter rocks than the ocean floors. Beneath the crust is the mantle, which is probably slightly liquid and moves very slowly. This movement is gradually shifting the continents and the ocean floors. The evidence of this today is in earthquakes and volcanic eruptions. Geologists believe that millions of years ago the continents were joined together, and have gradually moved apart.

The core of the Earth is thought to be partly molten and partly solid. It is probably mainly made of iron and nickel. Like the mantle, the core is almost certainly moving – and its movement may make the Earth act like a magnet, causing a compass needle to point north.

Climate and Vegetation

All life depends on water, and water comes from rain. This map shows the average amount of rain different parts of the world receive in a year. Compare it with the map of mountains and vegetation inside the covers. Some of the world's wet areas are near the Equator. Here, rain falls all through the year – there are storms and downpours nearly every day, and it is always hot. The natural vegetation is luxuriant *rain forest*, with tall trees and dangling creepers.

The world's driest places are hot *deserts* found near the two *Tropics*. Years may pass with little or no rain, but when storms do come, plants can spring up overnight.

Between the rain forest and the deserts are areas where it rains only at certain times of the year. In Asia, heavy rain falls during the *monsoon*, and the monsoon forests have hardwood trees like teak which lose their leaves in the dry season. Grass and bamboo flourish, too. In Africa and South America, the vegetation is called *savanna*. Where the wet season is quite long, there are plenty of trees and some grass. But where the wet season is short, the savanna is mainly grassland, dotted with

trees that can withstand the long dry season.

Away from the Tropics, the climate gets steadily colder towards the Poles. Near the tropical deserts it is still warm in the winter, as around the Mediterranean Sea. Here, and in similar parts of the world such as central Chile and central California, it rains in winter, and the summers are hot and sunny. The centres of the continents, far from the coast, are dry and have very cold winters. Parts are true desert, other areas are grasslands which

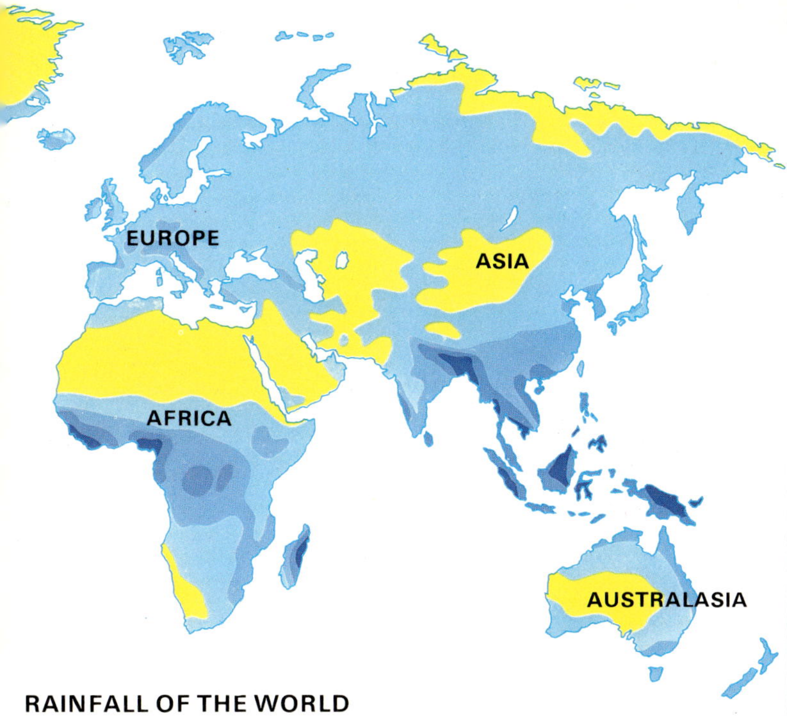

RAINFALL OF THE WORLD

are sometimes called steppes or prairies. Places facing winds blowing from the oceans, such as the Atlantic coast of Western Europe, are milder and wetter. In this part of the world the natural vegetation is deciduous forest in the warmer lands, but often most of this has been cleared for farming.

Vast areas of coniferous forest stretch across the cold northern lands. Trees are smaller and fewer towards the north, where there are biting winds and long cold winters. The vegetation this far north is *tundra* – mosses, lichens and low plants which can survive the cold. It snows rather than rains but there is plenty of water in the summer when the snow melts. Although the topsoil thaws, the frozen soil beneath prevents water draining away, so creating a vast marshy landscape where insects thrive. Near the Poles, permanent snow and ice take over. In the winter months it is always dark; in the summer it is always light but even the ever-present sun cannot melt the ice-caps.

World Facts and Figures

HIGHEST MOUNTAINS

Asia	m
Everest (Himalaya-Nepal/Tibet)	8848
Godwin Austen (Pakistan/India)	8611
Kanchenjunga (Himalaya-Nepal/Sikkim)	8597
Makalu (Himalaya-Nepal/Tibet)	8470
Dhaulagiri (Himalaya-Nepal)	8172
Nanga Parbat (Himalaya-India)	8126
Annapurna (Himalaya-Nepal)	8075
South America	
Aconcagua (Andes-Argentina)	6960
North America	
McKinley (Alaska-USA)	6194
Africa	
Kilimanjaro (Tanzania)	5895
Europe	
Elbruz (Caucasus-USSR)	5633
Mont Blanc (Alps-France)	4810
Antarctica	
Vinson Massif	5139
Australasia	
Wilhelm (Bismarck Range New Guinea)	4694

LONGEST RIVERS

	km
Nile (Africa)	6670
Amazon (S. America)	6437
Mississippi-Missouri-Red Rock (N. America)	6231
Yenisei (USSR)	5540
Yangtze (China)	5470
Ob-Irtysh (USSR)	5150
Zaire* (Africa)	4828
Lena (USSR)	4828
Amur (Asia)	4506
Hwang Ho (China)	4345
Mekong (SE. Asia)	4184
Niger (Africa)	4000

*Formerly Congo River

▲ **Largest desert:** sand dunes in the Sahara, in southern Morocco.

LARGEST LAKES

	sq km
Caspian Sea (USSR/Iran)	438,695
Superior (USA/Canada)	82,409
Victoria Nyanza (Africa)	69,484
Aral (USSR)	67,770
Huron (USA/Canada)	59,570
Michigan (USA)	58,016
Baikal (USSR)	34,180
Tanganyika (Africa)	31,999
Great Bear (Canada)	31,598
Malawi* (Africa)	28,490

*Also called Lake Nyasa

OCEANS

	sq km
Pacific	181,000,000
Atlantic	106,000,000
Indian	73,490,000
Arctic	14,350,000

DESERTS

	sq km
Sahara	8,400,000
Australian Desert	1,550,000
Arabian Desert	1,300,000
Gobi	1,040,000
Kalahari	520,000

▲ **Highest waterfall:** part of the Angel Falls, Venezuela.

▲ **Highest mountain:** the peak of Everest above Khumbu glacier.

MAJOR WATERFALLS

Highest	**metres**
Angel Falls (Venezuela)	979
Tugela Falls (South Africa)	948
Yosemite Falls (California)	739
Greatest Volume	**m^3/sec**
Niagara (N. America)	6,000

LARGEST ISLANDS

	sq km
Greenland (N. Atlantic)	2,175,600
New Guinea (SW. Pacific)	794,090
Borneo (SW. Pacific)	751,078
Madagascar (Indian Ocean)	587,041
Baffin I. (Canadian Artic)	476,066
Sumatra (Indian Ocean)	431,982
Honshu (NW. Pacific)	230,822
Great Britain (N. Atlantic)	229,522
Ellesmere (Canadian Arctic)	198,393
Victoria I. (Canadian Arctic)	192,695

EARTH EXTREMES

Hottest shade temperature recorded: 57·7°C at Al'Aziziyah, Libya, on 13.9.22

Coldest temperature recorded −88·3°C at Vostock, Antarctica, on 24.8.60

Highest annual rainfall: 11,680 mm at Mt Waialeale, Hawaii

Most rain in one month: 9300 mm at Cherrapunji, India, in July 1861

Driest place on earth: Arica, Chile, averages 0·76 mm of rain per year

Most snow in one year: 31,102 mm on Mt Rainier, Washington State, USA, 1971–2

Greatest ocean depth: 11,033 mm, Marianas trench, Pacific Ocean

Greatest tides: 16·3 m Bay of Fundy, Nova Scotia, Canada

Strongest surface wind recorded: 372 km/h at Mt Washington, N.H., USA, in 1934

Deepest gorge: 24,000 m, Hells Canyon, Idaho, USA

Longest gorge: 349 km, Grand Canyon, Arizona, USA

Highest navigated lake: Titicaca, Peru/Bolivia, 3810 m above sea level

Deepest lake: Baikal, Siberia, USSR, 1940 m

The World's Population

There are probably more than 4500 million people in the world, though an exact count is impossible. This means that there are only about 30 people to every square kilometre of land. But 20% of the Earth's surface is too dry to support many people; another 20% is too cold; 20% is too rugged and mountainous; and nearly 20% is dense tropical forest. That leaves only 20% of the Earth's surface to support the vast majority of the world's people. The map shows that as a result, some areas are very crowded indeed. These are the parts of the world with reasonably fertile land and a reasonably reliable water supply, where farming is possible.

Only a few parts of the world are really densely populated: parts of South and East Asia, and the industrialised parts of Western Europe and the USA. Few other areas seem crowded, except for the big cities.

Through most of history, the world's population has increased steadily but slowly. Population increases when there are more births than deaths. In the last 200 years, the population of the world has leapt from 800 to over 4500 million. This is because medical science has been able to conquer many killer diseases,

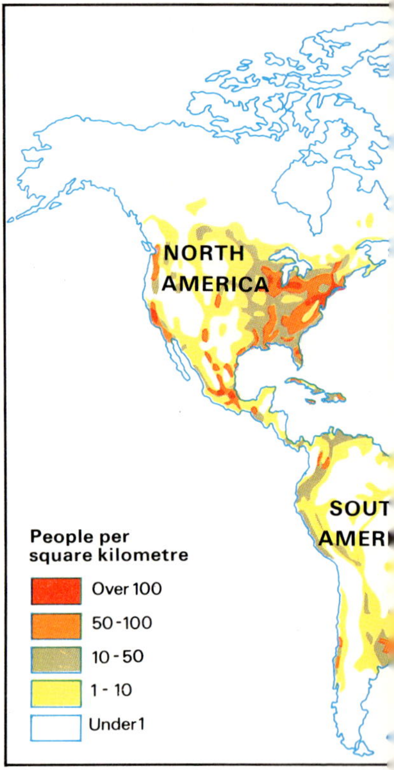

such as smallpox and cholera. So, although parents are actually producing *fewer* babies now than in the past, more of them live to grow up and have children of their own. The populations of Africa, Asia and Central and South America are increasing rapidly. Many countries in these continents have a 'young' population, with nearly half of their people under 15 years of age. The growth of population is much slower in North America, Europe and the USSR, and most of Australasia.

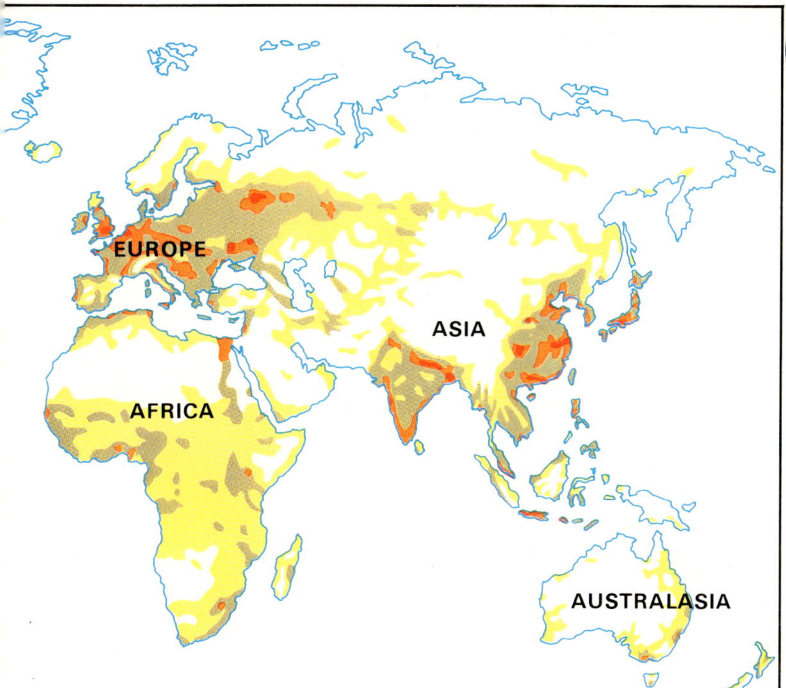

POPULATION DENSITY OF THE WORLD

POPULATION DENSITY

Population density means the number of people living in a square kilometre of land if the population of a country was evenly spread over the whole area. Figures = people per square kilometre.

Ten most crowded*		**Ten least crowded***	
Singapore	4262	Mongolia	1·1
Malta	1076	Botswana	1·4
Bangladesh	656	Mauritania	1·7
Mauritius	476	Libya	1·8
Taiwan	475	Australia	1·9
South Korea	401	Iceland	2·3
Netherlands	351	Gabon	2·5
Belgium	326	Surinam	2·5
Japan	322	Canada	2·5
Lebanon	320	Central African Republic	3·3

*The crowded territories of Macao, Hong Kong and Puerto Rico are not included as they are not independent nations.

*The empty lands of Greenland and Antarctica are not included as they are not independent nations.

East, West

Newspaper reports often divide the world into East and West. 'The East' usually refers to the Communist countries of Eastern Europe, the USSR and China. 'The West' refers to Western Europe, USA, Canada, Australia and their allies. These groups of countries (apart from China) are the developed countries of the world. Most of the rest of the world is still struggling to develop – these developing countries are sometimes called the Third World. Most of Central and South America, Africa, and southern Asia are the Third World.

▼ **This map** shows the developed 'North', the developing 'South' and the least developed countries in the world.

North, South

The division between the North and the South of the world is becoming more important. The map shows the dividing line – Australia and New Zealand are included in the North because of their wealth. The countries of 'The North' are rich in terms of industrial output. Most people living in these countries earn a good wage and have a varied diet. They have access to schools, doctors and other social services.

In 'The South' the story is different. The countries are struggling to feed their people and to find richer countries willing to pay a fair price for their exports. In these countries most people grow their own food, and many people do not have enough for a healthy diet.

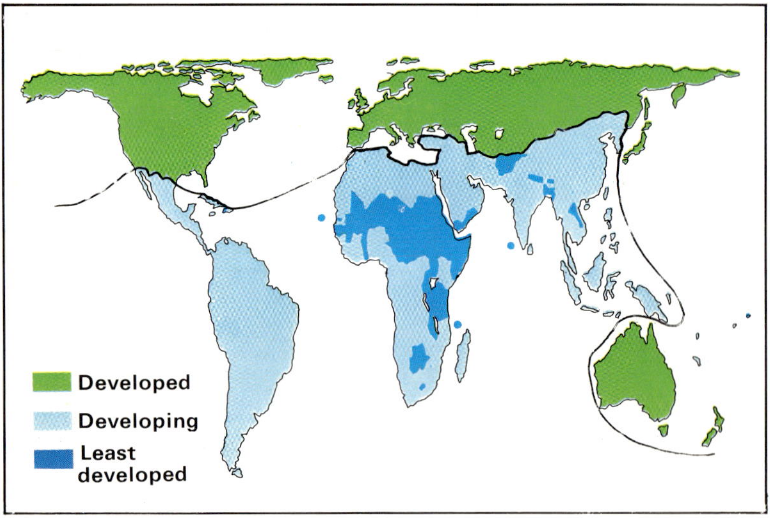

THE UNITED NATIONS

The United Nations (UN for short) has 155 member nations – all the independent countries except Switzerland, North and South Korea, Taiwan, and the 'mini-states' of Europe and the Pacific. Two republics of the USSR have separate membership. Each member has one vote in the General Assembly which meets at the UN Headquarters in New York.

Some UN agencies concerned with world development:

UNESCO – UN Education, Scientific and Cultural Organisation

UNICEF – UN International Children's Emergency Fund

FAO – Food and Agricultural Organisation

WHO – World Health Organisation

World Bank – for lending money

ILO – International Labour Organisation

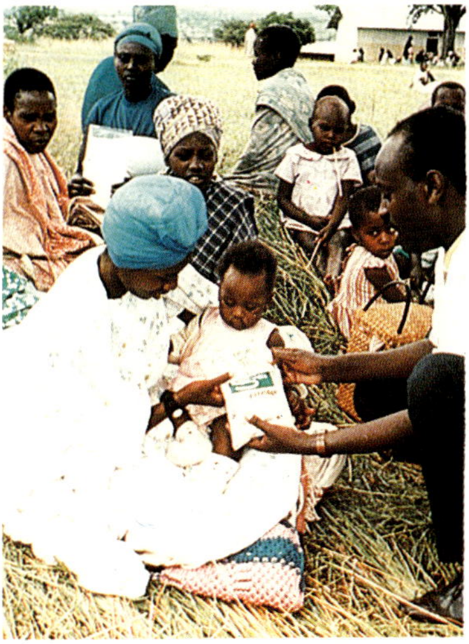

◀ **A UNICEF worker,** in Uganda, teaches mothers to prepare nourishing food.

RICH AND POOR COUNTRIES

Some ways of comparing countries are shown in this chart.

Column 1 shows **Adult Literacy:** the percentage of adults aged 15 and over who can read and write.

Column 2 shows **Life expectancy at Birth:** an average figure for how long people can expect to live (this will be low if lots of babies die, though in every country some people live to old age).

Column 3 shows **Gross National Product per person** in US dollars. GNP is a measure of the total output of goods (for example crops, minerals, industrial goods) and services (for example banking, shipping). The total value is converted into US dollars, then divided by the population to get an idea of output value per person.

Country	1	2	3
	%	years	US$per person
USA	99	73	9770
UK	99	73	5720
Sweden	99	75	13520
Australia	99	71	8060
Bangladesh	26	49	90
Bolivia	73	49	510
Haiti	24	53	240
India	33	49	180
Malawi	25	47	180
Upper Volta	2	43	160

These and other statistics have been used by the United Nations to work out which are the least developed countries (shown on map opposite).

Countries of the World

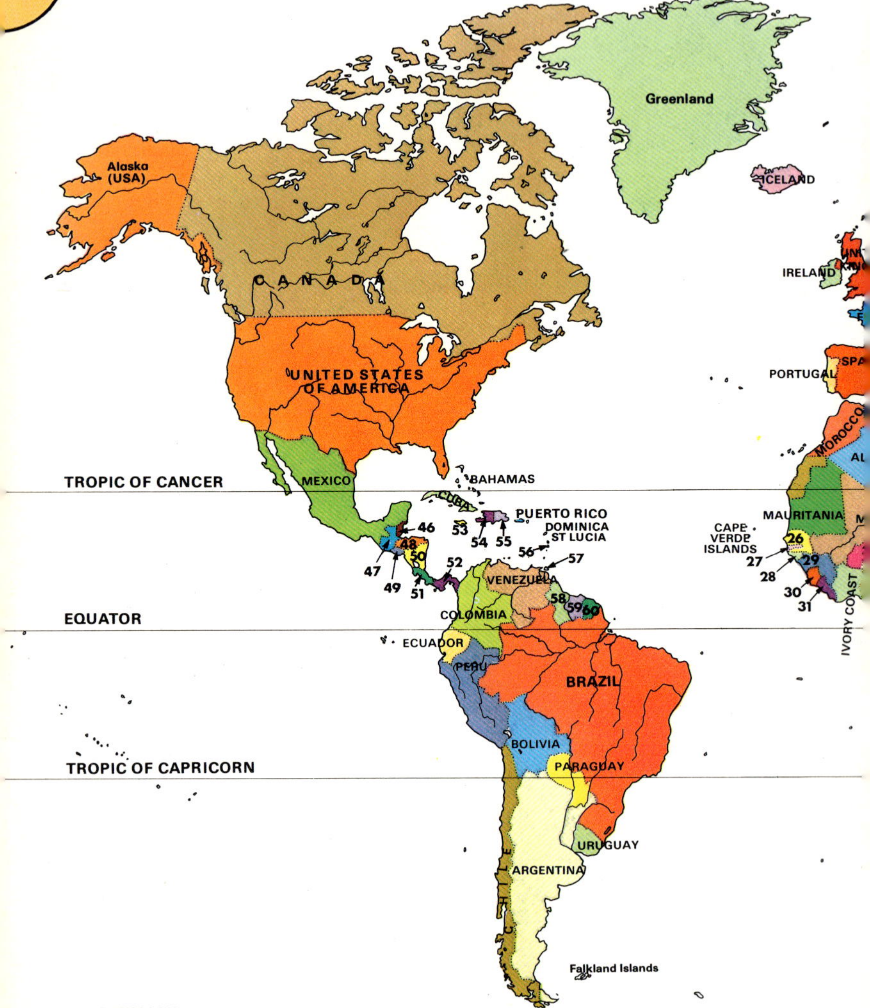

1 DENMARK
2 NETHERLANDS
3 BELGIUM
4 LUXEMBOURG
5 W. GERMANY
6 E. GERMANY
7 SWITZERLAND
8 AUSTRIA
9 CZECHOSLOVAKIA
10 HUNGARY
11 YUGOSLAVIA
12 ALBANIA
13 CYPRUS
14 LEBANON
15 ISRAEL
16 SYRIA
17 JORDAN
18 KUWAIT
19 BAHRAIN
20 UNITED ARAB EMIRATES
21 YEMEN
22 BHUTAN
23 BANGLADESH
24 KAMPUCHEA
25 TUNISIA
26 SENEGAL
27 GAMBIA
28 GUINEA-BISSAU
29 GUINEA
30 SIERRA LEONE

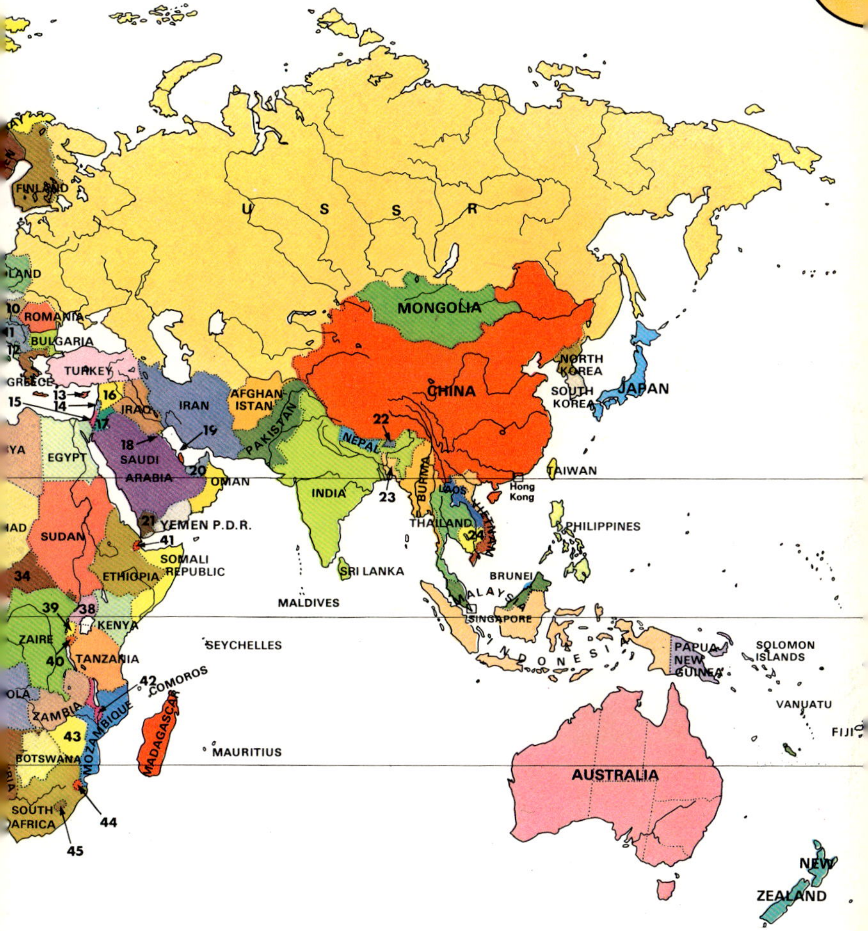

31 LIBERIA
32 UPPER VOLTA
33 TOGO
34 CENTRAL AFRICAN REPUBLIC
35 EQUATORIAL GUINEA
36 GABON
37 CAMEROON
38 UGANDA
39 RWANDA
40 BURUNDI
41 DJIBOUTI
42 MALAWI
43 ZIMBABWE
44 SWAZILAND
45 LESOTHO
46 BELIZE
47 GUATEMALA
48 HONDURAS
49 EL SALVADOR
50 NICARAGUA
51 COSTA RICA
52 PANAMA
53 JAMAICA
54 HAITI
55 DOMINICAN REPUBLIC
56 BARBADOS
57 TRINIDAD AND TOBAGO
58 GUYANA
59 SURINAM
60 FRENCH GUIANA

Making Maps

The surveyor carrying his heavy equipment and delicate instruments around the countryside can map the details of an area. But today, when large parts of the Earth's surface are mapped, cartographers rely on aeroplanes, satellites, computers and other complex equipment.

Overlapping air and satellite photographs are studied. Special machines enable the cartographer to trace the height of the land, and draw in all the features shown to produce photomaps. Remote areas can be mapped easily in this way. Satellite data is also used to produce weather maps, geology maps, land use maps, and detailed information about the whole surface of this planet.

▶ **A person** who draws maps is called a cartographer. This cartographer is adding details to a map of part of a town.

MAP PROJECTIONS

A globe is the only accurate map of the world. It is impossible to make a completely accurate map of the curved surface of the earth on a flat piece of paper. Try peeling the skin from an orange and laying it flat – there is always some distortion. Cartographers have struggled for centuries to make maps which conform as accurately as possible with the shape, area and scale of all or part of the world. To do so they use map projections. There are four main kinds:

Cylindrical projection

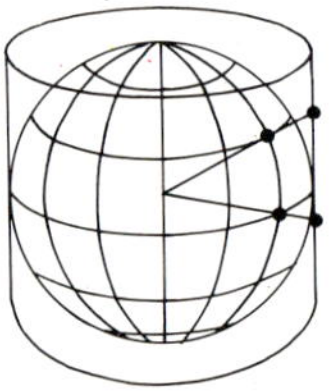

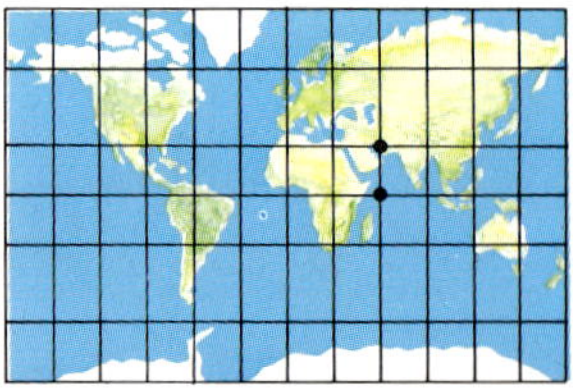

Cylindrical projections fit a cylinder of paper round the globe. Lines of latitude and longitude are straight. There is more exaggeration away from the Equator, but the shape of each small area is correct. The world maps on pages 12 and 20 and inside the covers are drawn on this kind of projection.

A variation of this is the **divided projection** where gaps are left in the oceans and the continents are drawn on segments. Lines of longitude curve towards the poles.

Conical projection

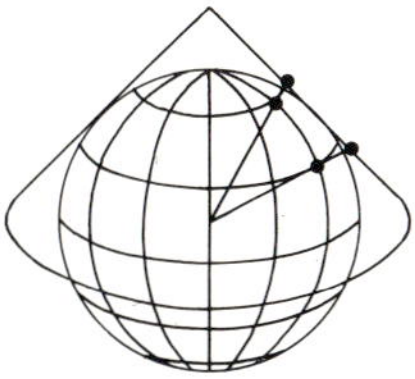

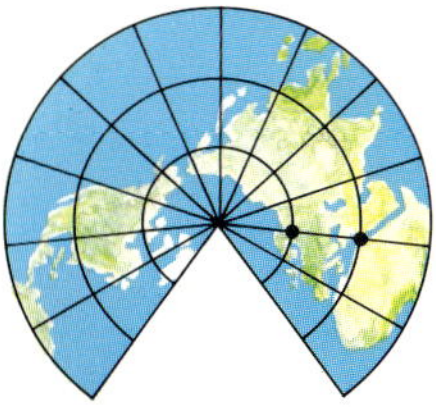

Polar zenithal projection

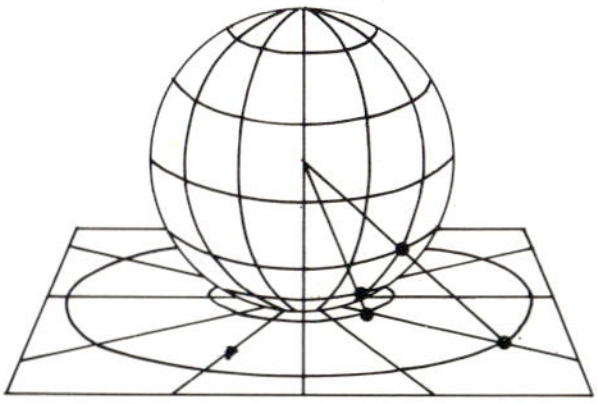

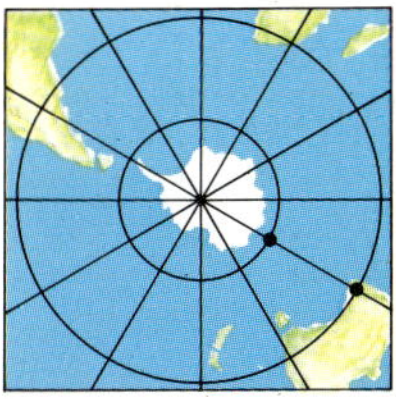

A **conical projection** is drawn as if a cone of paper was fitted round the globe. It is difficult to use for the whole world, but is a good projection for maps of countries.

Polar zenithal projections project the globe onto a flat piece of paper centred on the North or South Poles. There is more and more distortion away from the poles. The maps of the Arctic and Antarctic (pages 173 and 175) are drawn in this way.

Latitude and Longitude

On most globes you will see a network of curved lines: these are lines of latitude and longitude. They are labelled in degrees because they are measured by using angles at the centre of the earth. 1° (degree) is divided into 60′ (minutes). The lines parallel to the Equator are called lines of latitude. The Equator is 0°, and latitude is measured North and South of the Equator. The North Pole is at 90°N and the South Pole at 90°S.

Lines of longitude are sometimes called meridians. They are drawn from pole to pole. The 0° meridian passes through Greenwich, England. The other lines of longitude are measured East and West to the 180° meridian in the Pacific Ocean. The lines of latitude and longitude can be used to fix the position of any place on Earth. For example, the globe below shows part of Europe, Africa and America:

London is at about 51°N, 0°
Dakar is at about 14°N, 17°W
Rio de Janeiro is at 23°S, 43°W

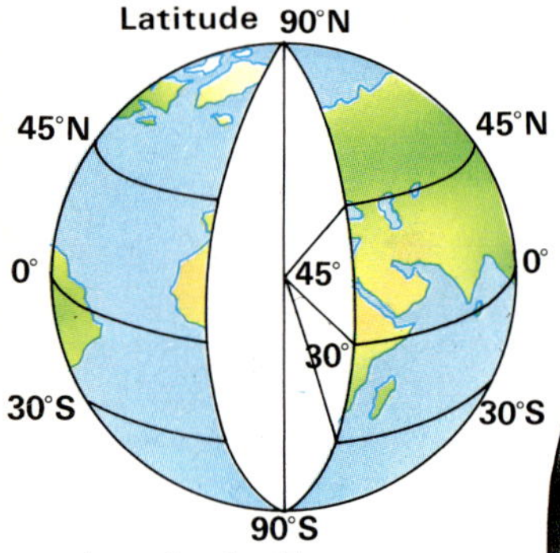

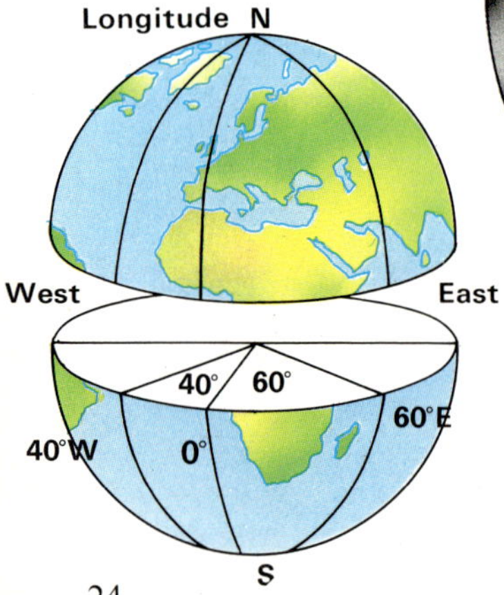

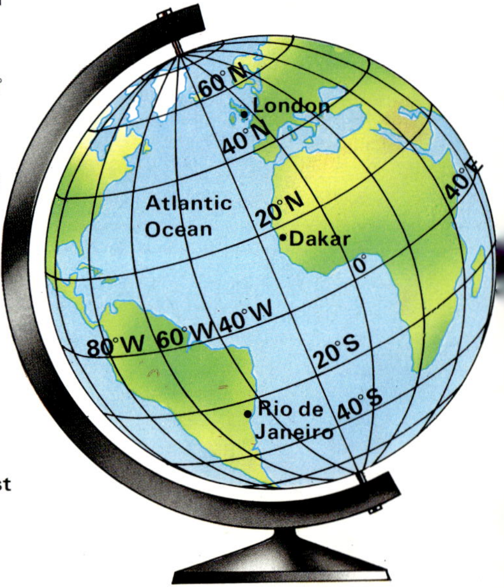

Earth Time

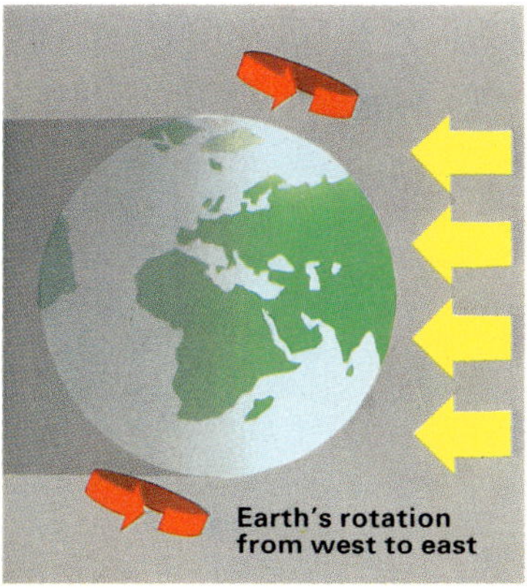

The Earth rotates on its axis once in 24 hours. This gives us day and night. At any one moment, part of the Earth is facing the Sun and people there have their clocks set at midday. On the opposite side of the Earth it is midnight.

Because the Earth rotates through 360° in 24 hours, there is one hour's time difference for every 15° of longitude. When it is midday in London (0°), it is 6 pm in the evening in Calcutta (90°E), but it is only sunrise at 6 am in Chicago (90°W). The map below shows these times. In 1884, an international conference agreed to divide the world into Time Zones. Each zone covers about 15° of longitude, but the boundaries follow national or state borders. The zones are shown on the map below. Within each zone, time is the same. But when you cross from one zone to another, you must change your watch by an hour. As you travel east, time is always ahead; westwards it is behind.

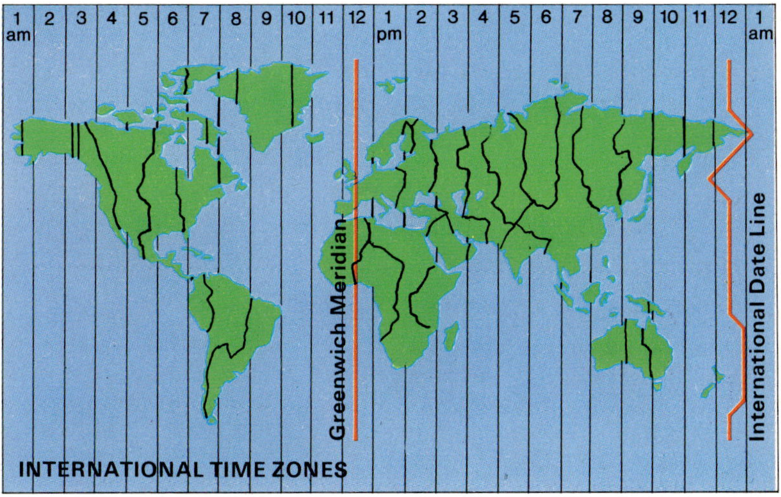

Europe

AREA:
10,531,000 sq km (including USSR west of the Urals and Caspian Sea and Turkey in Europe).
POPULATION:
695,000,000.
INDEPENDENT COUNTRIES:
32 (not including the USSR and Turkey).
HIGHEST POINT:
Mt Elbruz (5633 m).
LONGEST RIVERS:
Volga (2293 km), Danube (1700 km).
LARGEST LAKE:
Caspian Sea (438,695 sq km).
RICHEST COUNTRIES
(GNP per person – see p.19):
Switzerland ($16,440), Luxembourg ($14,510), Sweden ($13,520).
POOREST COUNTRIES:
Albania (no official figures, probably $840), Romania ($2340), Portugal ($2350).

Europe is a small continent – smaller in area than China or Brazil. But it has far more people than the continents of North America or Australasia, and is divided into many countries. In the past, many European countries had great empires, with *colonies* in all the other continents, and Europe grew rich from trade. Most of the colonies are now independent, but many still have close links with Europe.
The richest farmland, the main industrial areas and the large cities of Europe are found on the great *plain* which stretches from northern France to the USSR. To the north are mountains of very old rocks in Scandinavia and northern Britain. To the south are high mountain ranges: the Pyrenees, Alps, Carpathians and, further east, the Caucasus.

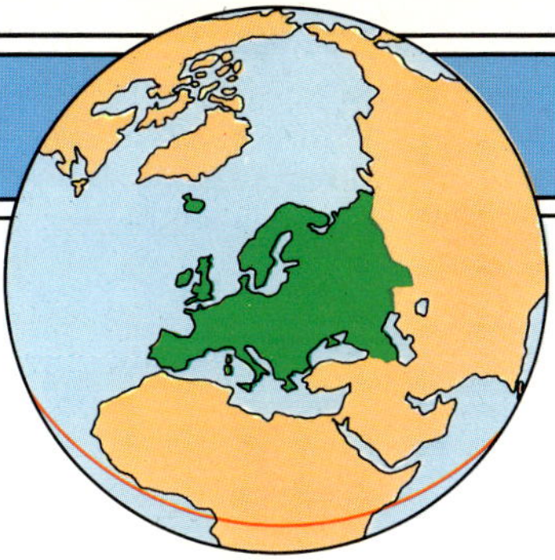

◀ **France:** centre of a small French town.

▲ **St Peter's,** Vatican City, Rome.

These mountains are still difficult to cross and often form the borders between countries. Further south are the hilly lands of southern Europe, around the Mediterranean Sea.

In the north and east of Europe, winters are long and cold. Western Europe has the most rain. Near the Mediterranean Sea there is plenty of hot weather and some rain in winter.

In the past European countries have fought over land and trade but it has been a peaceful continent since 1945. Today the biggest division in Europe is between the Communist countries in the East and the non-Communist countries in the West. Countries of both East and West Europe have formed groups to help each other: EEC, EFTA and COMECON.

Scandinavia and Finland

The five countries of Scandinavia and Finland are further north than almost any other inhabited area in the world. Northern Scandinavia is within the Arctic Circle, where the sun shines at midnight in the summer, but it is dark all day in winter.

Scandinavia and Finland have some of the most exciting scenery in the whole of Europe. Ice-caps and *glaciers* are found in the mountains of Norway and among the volcanoes of Iceland. These are just the small remains of huge *ice sheets* which spread out over much of Northern Europe during the *Ice Ages* in the past million years. In Norway the glaciers deepened mountain valleys; along the Norwegian coast these have been flooded by the sea to form huge inlets called *fiords*. The longest is Sogne Fiord (203 kilometres long). In Sweden and Finland, the great ice sheets scraped across lower land leaving large areas of thin soil and hundreds of lakes. *Moraine* was left behind also by the ice to form hummocks and ridges. In Denmark the ice sheets left behind rocks, gravels and clay. It is a low-lying country with fertile soil in some areas.

All these countries have quite small populations. The standard of living in each country is high, and few people are poor.

Hammerfest
ARCTIC OCEAN
Varanger Fiord
Tromsö
Narvik
LOFOTEN ISLANDS
Torne
2117m
Kiruna
Gallivare
Lule
Lulea
Oulu
USSR
Ume
Skelleftea
FINLAND
Umea
SWEDEN
Vaasa
Kuopio
Jyväskylä
Sundsvall
Ljusnan
GULF OF BOTHNIA
Pori (Bjorneborg)
Tampere
Lahti
Gavle
Klar
Dal
Turku
Helsinki
Västeras
Uppsala
GULF OF FINLAND
Orebro
Eskilstuna
Stockholm
Karlstad
Kilometres
0 50. 100 150 200 250
N
0 50 100 150
Miles
Norrköping
Linköping
Lake Vattern
Jonköping
GOTLAND
BALTIC SEA
BORNHOLM

FACTS AND FIGURES

Denmark

Finland

Iceland

Country (language)	Area (in sq km)	Population	Capital (population)	Highest point
DENMARK (Danish)	45,069	5,175,000	Copenhagen (654,00)	173 m in Jutland
FINLAND (Finnish, Swedish)	337,009	4,829,000	Helsinki (893,000)	Haltia, 1328 m
ICELAND (Icelandic)	103,000	234,000	Reykjavik (84,000)	Oraefajokull, 2119 m
NORWAY (Norwegian)	324,219	4,138,000	Oslo (455,000)	Galdhopiggen, 2472 m
SWEDEN (Swedish)	449,964	8,347,000	Stockholm (654,000)	Mt Kebne-kaise 2117 m

Norway

Sweden

Currency	Main exports
Krone	Machinery, animals, meat, dairy produce, eggs, metals, metal goods
Markka	Paper, paper-board, machinery wood and woodpulp
Krona	Fish products
Krone	Machinery, paper, metals, metal products, oil, animal products
Krona	Machinery, cars, metals, metal goods, timber and timber products

CLIMATE

Bergen (Norway)

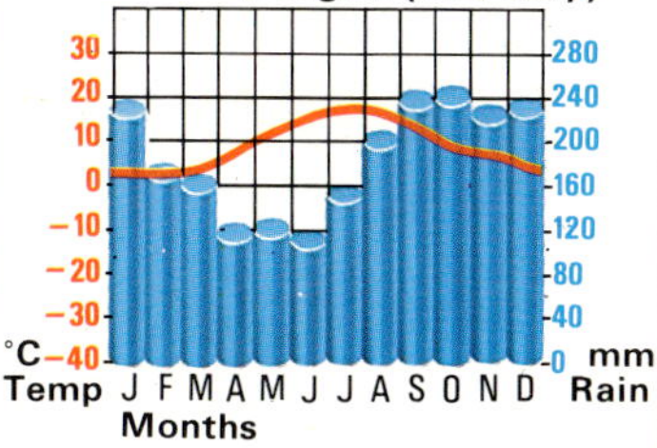

Bergen is on the coast of Norway. Although it is further north than Scotland, the weather is surprisingly mild and there is plenty of rain. Bergen benefits from the North Atlantic Drift – an ocean *current* that brings warm water across the Atlantic from the Caribbean. So winds from the sea are mild and moist. The warm current keeps the coast of Norway ice-free even in midwinter. Where it mixes with cold currents from the Arctic Ocean, the sea is rich with food and there are lots of fish.

◀ **Norway:** one of the arms of Sogne Fiord where the sea reaches far inland.

▼ **Sweden:** ice-hockey in the low winter sun in a suburb of Stockholm.

PRODUCTS

Farming: Very difficult in most of Scandinavia and Finland because a great deal of the land is high, much of the lower land has poor soil and, in the north and east, the winters are long and cold. In Iceland and Norway, the weather is damp and cloudy too. Only 1% of Iceland is cultivated: 3% of Norway; 8% of Sweden and 9% of Finland. It is the southernmost low land that is always most important for farming. Hay and root crops are grown.

In Denmark the situation is different and 90% of the land is farmed. Fodder crops for cattle and pigs are especially important. Dairy products, pork and bacon are major exports.

Fishing: Iceland's chief industry; important also in Norway and Denmark.

Forestry: Especially important in Finland, Sweden and Norway. About 70% of Finland is forest, 60% of Sweden and 20% of Norway, but trees grow very slowly in the far north. These three countries are major exporters of woodpulp and paper. Boards, plywood, veneers, charcoal and matches are also made.

Industry: Many industries process raw materials – fish in Iceland; forest products in Sweden, Finland and Norway; farm products in Denmark. Other industries are based on mineral resources: Sweden has valuable iron ore deposits used for high quality steel goods from cars and ships to ball-bearings and cutlery. Norway has iron ore, copper, lead and zinc used in making metal products and machinery. Finland manufactures machinery and transport equipment. Chemical products are also made in Sweden and Norway using cheap hydro-electricity and North Sea oil.

GOVERNMENT

All these five countries have democratic governments. Norway, Sweden and Denmark each have a king or queen. Iceland and Finland are Republics. Sweden and Finland are neutral countries; Iceland, Norway and Denmark are allied to the UK and other European countries and the USA in NATO (North Atlantic Treaty Organisation).

Sweden: Independent for many centuries, it used to rule Finland (until 1809) and Norway (from 1814 to 1905).

Denmark: Once ruled Norway (until 1814) and Iceland (until 1944). It continued to rule Greenland (now self-governing) and the Faeroe Islands. Denmark is the only Scandinavian country in the Common Market.

Finland: Independent from Russian rule in 1917. The Finnish language is quite different from the other Scandinavian languages: it came from Central Asia. The Finnish name for Finland is 'Suomi', but the Swedish name 'Finland' is also used.

THE LAPPS

Lappland is the part of Scandinavia and Finland north of the Arctic circle. There are only about 40,000 Lapps altogether. Once they were nomadic hunters and fishermen. Now some work in towns, mines, factories and forests. Many are reindeer-herders: the reindeer graze the tundra and provide good meat.

▼ **Iceland** has mostly been built by volcanic activity and there are still many active volcanoes, as well as geysers, hot springs and boiling mud pools. Power stations generate electricity using the heat from hot rocks in the Earth's crust. Despite the heat, Iceland has lots of glaciers – the longest is Vatnajokull (141 km).

THE VIKINGS

Vikings were the ancestors of today's Scandinavians. Over a thousand years ago they set out in their 'longships' to raid and settle in other countries. They travelled north to the Faeroe Islands, Iceland and Greenland – some may have reached North America. They also raided and occupied parts of Russia and central Europe, and settled along the coast of northern Europe. England had a Danish king – Canute – in 1016. The Norsemen who lived in France were called Normans, and later they conquered England.

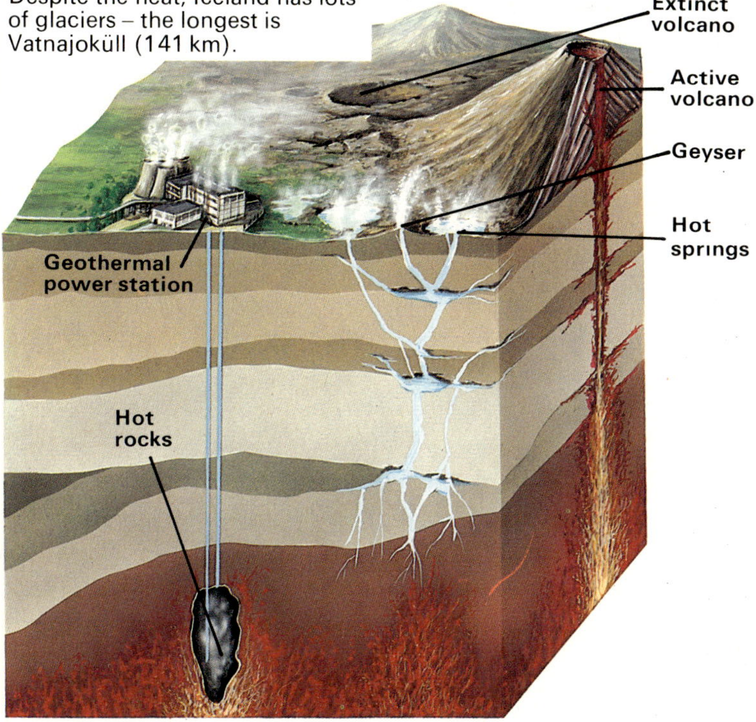

Netherlands, Belgium and Luxembourg

Netherlands

Luxembourg

Belgium

The Netherlands, Belgium and Luxembourg are the three smallest countries in the EEC (the Common Market), but they are densely populated and have important industries. The historic towns of Bruges and Ghent in Belgium and Amsterdam in the Netherlands attract many visitors.

These three countries are sometimes called Benelux and their close co-operation was an example that helped form the Common Market. Now the EEC headquarters are in Brussels. The Low Countries is another name for these countries because all of the Netherlands and most of Belgium are very low-lying. These countries are at the mouth of the Rhine and other smaller rivers. For centuries the ports here have traded with Europe and the rest of the world via the rivers and the North Sea. Today, Rotterdam is the largest port in the world.

▼ **Belgium:** the market place and rooftops of Bruges.

NORTH SEA
Groningen
Lake
Ijssel
Haarlem
Amsterdam
Ijssel
Enschede
NETHERLANDS
Leiden
s Gravenhage
(The Hague)
Utrecht
Arnhem
Rotterdam
Waal
Rhine
Dorarecht
Nijmegen
Maas
s Hertogenbosch
Breda
Tilburg
Eindhoven
stend
Bruges
Antwerp
Ghent
WEST GERMANY
Lys
Heerlen-Kerkrase
Maastricht
Brussels
Scheldt
Liege
BELGIUM
Meuse
Sambre
FRANCE
Ardennes
LUXEMBOURG
Luxembourg
0 Kilometres
50
0 Miles
30
N

BELGIUM

Land: Mostly lowland, with dunes and polders near the coast. South of rivers Sambre and Meuse are the Ardennes – forested hills with deep valleys.
Farming: Mostly on small farms run part-time by families. Market gardening important on polders and near main towns. Elsewhere cereals, root crops, hops and flax important.
Mining: Coal was once very important in Sambre-Meuse valley – the basis of iron and steel industries and engineering. Now the coal seams are exhausted and mines have closed causing unemployment. Most coal now comes from Kempenland, on Dutch border.
Industry: Includes iron and steel, textiles, glass-making, food processing, metals, paper, oil and a full range of engineering. Main exports are industrial goods.

LUXEMBOURG

A Grand Duchy: the smallest and richest country in the Common Market. Forested hills in the north are part of the Ardennes; rest is lowland known as the Bon Pays or Gutland (Good Land).
Farming: Mainly mixed farming (crops and animals) with vines in the Moselle Valley.
Industry: Most important is iron and steel, with related chemicals and engineering. Iron ore mined on the southern border; coal is imported. Hydro-electric power is generated in northern hills.

FACTS AND FIGURES

BELGIUM
Area: 30,513 sq km
Population: 9,941,000
Capital (population): Brussels (1,009,000)
Official languages: Flemish, French
Highest point: Botrange, 694 m
Currency: Belgian franc
Main exports: Chemicals, vehicles, machinery, iron and steel

LUXEMBOURG
Area: 2586 sq km
Population: 360,000
Capital (population): Luxembourg City (80,000)
Official languages: French, Luxemburgish (a German dialect)
Highest point: Bourgplatz, 559 m
Currency: Franc
Main exports: See Belgium

THE NETHERLANDS
Area: 40,844 sq km
Population: 14,324,000
Capital (population): Amsterdam (717,000); The Hague is the Seat of Government
Offical language: Dutch
Currency: Guilder
Highest point: Vaalserberg, 321 m
Main exports: petroleum, chemicals, food and animals, machinery

▶ **Dutch Polders:** the pumping station pumps water from the drainage channels up to the main canal.

NETHERLANDS

Land: Its name means 'low lands'. About 40% of the country consists of *polders* and coastland reclaimed from the sea and is below sea level at high tide. Reclamation began in 13th century. Polders are surrounded by *dykes* (banks) to keep out the sea and criss-crossed by drainage ditches. Water once removed by windpumps now by diesel pumps. Major reclamation schemes include the Zuider Zee and Delta projects. The Zuider Zee was turned into the freshwater lake Ijssel and polders with 2260 square kilometres of new land. The Delta Project involved damming all but two exits of the Rhine-Maas-Scheldt delta. This scheme protects land from floods and creates a freshwater lake and 150 square kilometres of new land.

Farming: Intensive and highly mechanised. Rich polder lands are important for dairy farming (butter and cheese exported); land near the sandy coast for horticulture (bulbs, vegetables, salad crops). Natural gas is used to heat greenhouses. Arable farming on land in east and south which was once heathland.

Industry: Very important for employment and for exports. Main industrial areas are near ports as most industry is based on imports. The chief industries are metal and engineering products, followed by the food and tobacco industries which use some home-grown produce; also electrical goods – main factory at Eindhoven belonging to Philips – and diamond-cutting, a specialized industry in Amsterdam.

The British Isles

United Kingdom

Ireland

There are two countries in the British Isles: the United Kingdom and the Republic of Ireland. The United Kingdom consists of Great Britain (England, Wales and Scotland) and Northern Ireland. Scotland has some different laws from England and Wales, but there is no Scottish parliament: the laws are enacted in London. Wales has its own language – Welsh. It is a Celtic language, like Gaelic (spoken in north-western parts of Scotland) and Erse (spoken in Ireland).

The Republic of Ireland became independent in 1922. Three and a half million people live there today, only half the number that lived there in the 1930s. Famines, unemployment and other problems have forced many Irish people to emigrate to other countries. The capital is Dublin.

UNITED KINGDOM
Area: 244,046 sq km (not including Isle of Man and Channel Islands)
Population: 55,670.000
Capital (population): London (6,969,000)
Highest point: Ben Nevis 1347 m
Official language: English
Currency: Sterling pound
Main exports: Manufactured goods

IRELAND
Area: 70,283 sq km
Population: 3,366,000
Capital (population): Dublin (545,000)
Highest point: Carrantuohill, 1042 m
Official languages: English, Irish
Currency: Irish pound (punt)
Main exports: Dairy products, meat, meat products, beer, whiskey

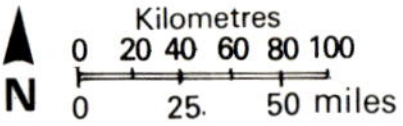

ORKNEY
ISLANDS
SHETLAND ISLANDS
John o'
Groats
HEBRIDES
North West Highlands
Inverness
Loch Ness
Dee
Aberdeen
Ben Nevis
1347m
Grampians
Tay
Dundee
SCOTLAND
Loch
Lomond
Glasgow
Edinburgh
Clyde
Tyne
Londonderry
NORTHERN
IRELAND
Belfast
Pennines
Eden
Newcastle
NORTH
SEA
Lake
District
ISLE OF MAN
GREAT
BRITAIN
York
Hull
Leeds
Manchester
Liverpool
Sheffield
Dublin
IRISH
SEA
Snowdon
1086m
Trent
Nottingham
Wicklow
Mts
Cambrian Mts
Leicester
The
Fens
Norwich
Great
Yarmouth
Barrow
Birmingham
Severn
Ouse
Cambridge
Avon
WALES
ENGLAND
Cotswolds
Oxford
Chiltern Hills
Swansea
Thames
London
Cardiff
Bristol
Bath
North Downs
Canterbury
Dover
Exmoor
Southampton
Portsmouth
Brighton
Bournemouth
Isle of Wight
Dartmoor
Plymouth
ISLES OF
SCILLY
Land's
End
ENGLISH CHANNEL
FRANCE

INDUSTRY AND FARMING

Britain:
Minerals: Coal and iron ore are chief resources: older industrial areas are on coalfields.
Industry: Textiles, iron and steel, heavy engineering, shipbuilding and chemicals are very important. Imports of raw materials and food supplement home supplies. Major ports have important processing industries.
Energy: Electricity mainly generated from coal and oil. Some *hydro-electricity* in Scotland and Wales. Electricity is important for new industries in many towns in south and east England as in Ireland. Oil and natural gas from North Sea important. Oil refineries and chemical industries on coast use local and imported oil.
Ireland:
Few minerals and far fewer manufacturing industries. Most industry concerned with processing raw materials from farming – dairying, flour mills, brewing, sugar and bacon processing.

Britain:
Land: Highland areas in north and west have the highest rainfall. Lowland in east and south has richer soil and drier climate.
Farming: Most of the land is farmed. Arable farming mainly in drier east (cereals, potatoes, sugar beet and vegetables). Pastoral farming important in west and north Britain (sheep, cattle, pigs).
Fishing: Important in coastal waters and North Atlantic.
Ireland:
Land: Hills surround central lowland, containing marshy land with many lakes and some rich farmland. Rainfall is heavy.
Farming: Most of the land is farmed and dairy farming and livestock rearing provide important exports (butter, cheese, meat and animals). Major crops include barley, hay, wheat, potatoes and sugar beet.

▼ **York** is a busy English county town. Many tourists visit the cathedral and museums.

COUNTIES OF BRITAIN

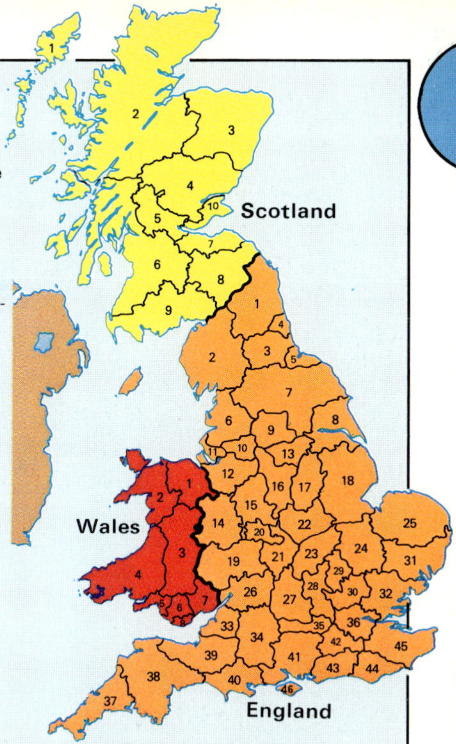

ENGLISH COUNTIES

Metropolitan counties	Administrative HQ
36 Greater London	—
10 Greater Manchester	—
	—
11 Merseyside	Liverpool
13 South Yorkshire	Barnsley
4 Tyne and Wear	Newcastle-upon-Tyne
20 West Midlands	Birmingham
9 West Yorkshire	Wakefield
Other counties	
33 Avon	Bristol
29 Bedfordshire	Bedford
35 Berkshire	Reading
28 Buckinghamshire	Aylesbury
24 Cambridgeshire	Cambridge
12 Cheshire	Chester
5 Cleveland	Middlesbrough
37 Cornwall and the Isles of Scilly	Truro
2 Cumbria	Carlisle
16 Derbyshire	Matlock
38 Devon	Exeter
40 Dorset	Dorchester
3 Durham	Durham
44 East Sussex	Lewes
32 Essex	Chelmsford
26 Gloucestershire	Gloucester
41 Hampshire	Winchester
19 Hereford & Worcester	Worcester
30 Hertfordshire	Hertford
8 Humberside	Kingston upon Hull
46 Isle of Wight	Newport
45 Kent	Maidstone
6 Lancashire	Preston
22 Leicestershire	Leicester
18 Lincolnshire	Lincoln
25 Norfolk	Norwich
23 Northamptonshire	Northampton
1 Northumberland	Morpeth
7 North Yorkshire	Northallerton
17 Nottinghamshire	Nottingham
27 Oxfordshire	Oxford
14 Shropshire	Shrewsbury
39 Somerset	Taunton
15 Staffordshire	Stafford
31 Suffolk	Ipswich
42 Surrey	Kingston upon Thames
21 Warwickshire	Warwick
43 West Sussex	Chichester
34 Wiltshire	Trowbridge

NORTHERN IRELAND

For administration, the Province is divided into 26 districts, replacing the 6 Counties.

WELSH COUNTIES

Counties	Administrative HQ
1 Clwyd	Mold
4 Dyfed	Carmarthen
7 Gwent	Cwmbran
2 Gwynedd	Caernarfon
6 Mid-Glamorgan	Cardiff
3 Powys	Llandrindod Wells
8 South Glamorgan	Cardiff
5 West Glamorgan	Swansea

SCOTTISH REGIONS

Counties	Administrative HQ
8 Borders	Newton St Boswells
5 Central	Stirling
9 Dumfries & Galloway	Dumfries
10 Fife	Glenrothes
3 Grampian	Aberdeen
2 Highland	Inverness
7 Lothian	Edinburgh
6 Strathclyde	Glasgow
4 Tayside	Dundee
1 Western Isles	Stornoway

Germany-West and East

Germany was one country until the end of World War II when it was divided into four zones. The UK, USA and France occupied the three zones in the west; the USSR occupied the eastern zone. The eastern zone is now the separate country of East Germany or the DDR and it is still closely linked with the USSR. The rest of the country, and part of Berlin, now forms West Germany.

West Germany is the only European country with more than 60 million people – apart from the USSR. It is a rich country with many modern industries. East Germany is poorer than West Germany, but the richest and most industrialized country of Eastern Europe.

The lowlands in the north of the two Germanies are part of the North European Plain. In places there is rich farmland but there are large areas of marsh and sandy heath as well, formed by the *ice sheets* of the *Ice Ages*. Large rivers flow across the *plains* to wide *estuaries* opening onto the Baltic and North Sea. These rivers begin in the high land of the south where the forested hills and mountains are divided by deep valleys. The river Danube begins in the Black Forest and flows east to the Black Sea. The Black Forest is one of several highland areas bordering the river Rhine, which flows north. The highest land is in the Alps, on the border of Germany and Austria.

▼ **The River Rhine** flows northwards between hills with vineyards. Industrial cities have grown beside the river, and barges travel between the ports.

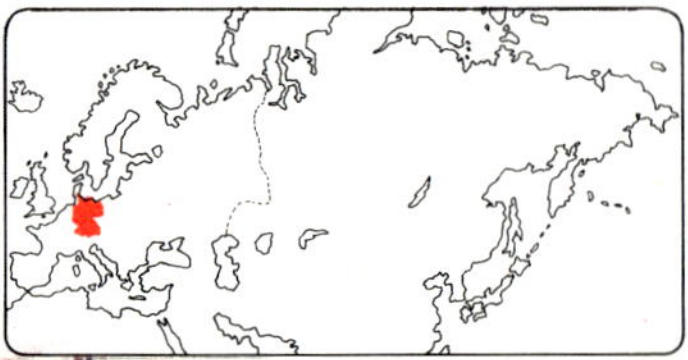

DENMARK
BALTIC SEA
NORTH SEA
etres
50
100
150
30
60
90
N
Kiel Canal
Kiel
Rostock
Lubeck
Hamburg
Elbe
Ems
ERLANDS
Bremen
POLAND
Oder
Aller
West Berlin
East Berlin
Weser
Hanover
Brunswick
Magdeburg
EAST GERMANY
Oder
Spree
Munster
Bielefeld
Harz Mts
Neisse
Elbe
Dortmund
Essen
Bochum
Ruhr
Halle
Wuppertal
Kassel
Leipzig
Dusseldorf
Cologne
Dresden
Bonn
Karl-Marx-Stadt
WEST GERMANY
Frankfurt
Wiesbaden
Mainz
Mosel
Main
CZECHOSLOVAKIA
Mannheim
Nuremberg
Saarbrucken
Rhine
Karlsruhe
Stuttgart
Danube
FRANCE
Black Forest
Augsburg
Inn
Munich
Freiburg
Alps
AUSTRIA
SWITZERLAND

FACTS AND FIGURES

WEST GERMANY
German Federal Republic
Area: 248,577 sq km
Population: 61,392,000
Capital (population): Bonn (286,000)
Largest city: West Berlin (1,902,000)
Highest point: Zugspitze, 2963 m
Official language: German
Currency: Deutschmark
Main exports: Manufactured goods, chemicals, coke, consumer goods

EAST GERMANY
German Democratic Republic (DDR)
Area: 108,178 sq km
Population: 16,748,000
Capital (population): East Berlin (1,134,000)
Highest point: Fichtelberg 1214 m
Official language: German
Currency: DDR mark
Main exports: Engineering goods, chemicals

WEST GERMANY

Minerals and Power: Coal is plentiful in the Ruhr and near Aachen. Oil and gas come from beneath northern plain. Other minerals include lignite (brown coal) and potash deposits.
Industry: One of the world's leading industrial nations. Main industrial area is the Ruhr: the greatest single industrial area in Europe. Here there are iron and steel works, and factories producing all kinds of metal goods (including cars), chemicals, textiles and other products. Engineering (general and electrical) employs the most people and produces main exports. Industries in all main towns and at North Sea ports.
Farming: Employs few people and provides few exports, but supplies two-thirds of Germany's food. The amount of farmland is decreasing as more is built on. Main crops include cereals, potatoes, sugar beet. In south: maize, fruit and vines.

West Germany

East Germany

BERLIN

Once the capital of the whole of Germany, Berlin was divided into zones of occupation in 1945. West Berlin remains a part of West Germany although it is over 150 km away from the rest of the country. It has more people than any other West German town and is separated from East Berlin by a wall. East Berlin has remained the capital of East Germany.

◀ **West Germany:** a farm in the Weser hills near Hanover.

▼ **East Germany:** Rostock is an important city. In the distance are part of the port and the shipyards.

EAST GERMANY

Minerals and Power: Huge deposits of lignite (soft brown coal) provide the main power source. Hard coal is only found in small quantities. Vast reserves of potash and some iron ore.
Industry: More industry in East Germany than in any other East European country. Engineering is the chief industry followed by chemicals, food processing, textiles. The most industrialized city is Berlin, followed by cities in the south near resources: Dresden, Leipzig and Karl-Marx-Stadt areas.
Farming: Most productive in the south, where soil is most fertile. The main crops here are wheat, barley, sugarbeet. Rye and potatoes are grown on poorer soils in the north. Some food has to be imported. Forests cover more than a quarter of the country.

Switzerland, Austria and Liechtenstein

Switzerland

Austria

The Alps cover large parts of these land-locked countries and attract many visitors in summer and winter. Spectacular bridges and tunnels take roads and railways through the mountains, linking northern and southern Europe.

In all these countries, many fast-flowing rivers have been dammed to generate *hydro-electric power*. Switzerland has few natural resources, yet it is one of the world's richest countries. Factories powered by electricity make small but valuable goods such as watches. Banks and offices are important as well as hotels for tourists.

Unlike Switzerland, Austria has some mineral resources, including iron ore and oil for industry, but tourism is important as well. Until 1918, Austria was the main part of a much larger country which included Hungary and many other areas of central Europe – the Austro-Hungarian Empire.

Two out of three Swiss people speak German as their first language. Others speak French, Italian or Romansch. Stamps and coins use the old Latin name Helvetia. CH on car plates means 'Confederatio Helvetia' (the Swiss Confederation).

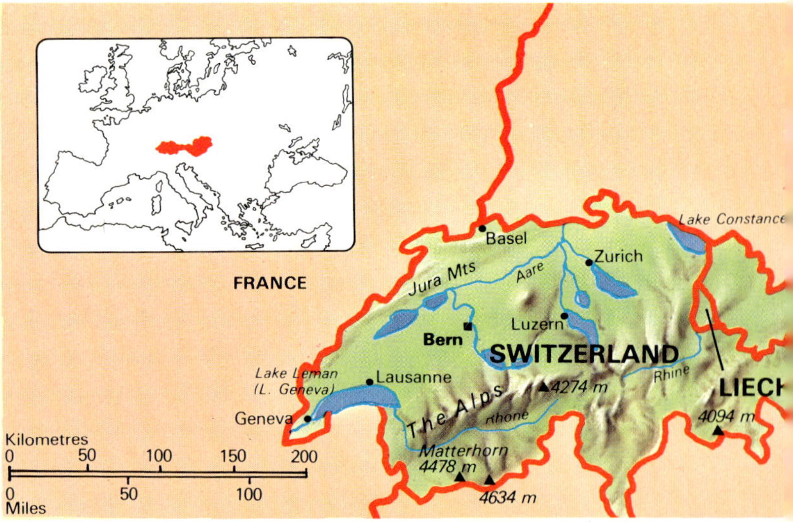

AUSTRIA
Area: 83,849 sq km
Population: 7,526,000
Capital (population): Vienna (1,615,000)
Highest point: Grossglockner, 3797 m
Official language: German
Currency: Schilling

SWITZERLAND
Area: 41,288 sq km
Population: 6,350,000
Capital (population): Bern (282,000)
Largest city: Zurich (707,000)
Highest point: Monte Rosa, 4634 m
Official languages: French German, Italian
Currency: Swiss franc

LIECHTENSTEIN
Area: 157 sq km
Population: 26,000
Capital (population): Vaduz (5000)
Official language: German
Currency: Swiss franc

▲ **Austria:** a chairlift takes tourists up to the high mountains.

France

France is the largest country in Europe except for the USSR. It also has the most varied landscape. In the north and west are low-lying plains which have cool weather for most of the year. In the east are the French Alps with Mont Blanc, Western Europe's highest mountain. In the south, are the high mountains of the Pyrenees on the Spanish border. The Massif Central is lower, but the scenery includes wild limestone hills and gorges and the cores of old volcanoes. These mountain areas have snow in the winter, but the Mediterranean coast has mild winters and hot, sunny summers.

At one time France was a kingdom, but it became a republic after the French Revolution in 1789. The slogan of the leaders of the revolution can still be found on every French coin: 'Liberté, Egalité, Fraternité' (Liberty, Equality and Brotherhood). France was invaded by Germany in 1871, 1914 and 1940, but most of the beautiful and historic towns and cities have survived. Now, France and Germany are allies in the Common Market.

France

Monaco

CHANNEL
Dunkerque
Calais
Boulogne
Roubaix
Lille
Valenciennes
Douai
BELGIUM
LUXEMBOURG
GERMANY
Dieppe
Somme
Amiens
Le Havre
Rouen
Ouise
Meuse
Seine
Reims
Metz
Marne
Nancy
Strasbourg
Paris
Chartres
Fontainebleau
Moselle
Vosges Mts
Le Mans
Orleans
Mulhouse
Saône
Loire
Dijon
Tours
FRANCE
SWITZERLAND
Jura Mts
Limoges
Lyon
Mt Blanc 4810m
Clermont-Ferrand
Mt Dore 1886m
Saint Étienne
Grenoble
Massif Central
ITALY
French Alps
Dordogne
Cévennes Mts
Rhône
Garonne
Nîmes
Avignon
Montpellier
Arles
Toulouse
Nice
MONACO
Cannes
Marseille
Toulon
Carcassonne
ANDORRA
MEDITERRANEAN SEA

FARMING

France is the biggest producer of food in Europe apart from the USSR. Most of northern and western France is fertile lowland where the main crops are wheat, barley, maize and sugarbeet.

Pastoral farming is also very important: French cheeses made from milk of cows, goats and sheep according to local recipes are famous. Another famous farm product is France's excellent wines: vineyards are found on south-facing hillsides in many regions.

Fruit and vegetables are also grown: oranges and lemons, apricots, peaches and other fruit near the Mediterranean and lower Rhône Valley; apples and pears in Normandy and other northern areas.

FACTS AND FIGURES

FRANCE
Area: 547,026 sq km
Population: 54,414,000
Capital (population): Paris (8,550,000).
Highest point: Mont Blanc, 4810 m
Official language: French
Currency: Franc
Main exports: Cars, chemicals, iron and steel, textiles and leather goods, electrical equipment, wine, cereals

MONACO
Area: 1·9 sq km (190 hectares)
Population: 25,000
Capital: Monaco
Official language: French
Currency: French franc
Income: Mainly from tourists and the casino in Monte-Carlo

▼ **Grapes for wine** are harvested in a vineyard near Dijon in eastern France.

▶ **The 21 administrative regions** use several of the names of the old provinces abolished in 1789.

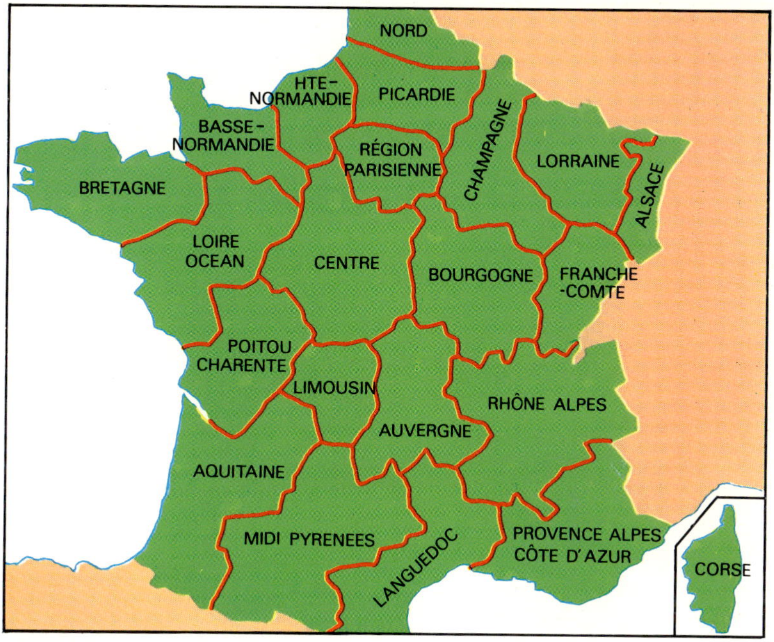

INDUSTRY

Minerals: Coal is mined in the north-east. Important iron ore deposits are found in Lorraine. Bauxite first mined in France (at Les Baux). Other minerals include uranium, potash and natural gas.
Energy: Coal, gas and *hydro-electric power* are important.
Industry: A wide range of manufacturing industries. Iron and steel works, once on the coalfield, are now at Dunkirk and Fos-sur-Mer near Marseille. French cars such as Renault, Peugeot and Citroen, are an important export. Chemicals are made on coalfields in the north-east, and in Paris and Lyon; oil refineries are at the coast (Dunkirk; lower Seine; near Marseille); textiles are traditionally important in Lille, and in Paris and Lyon. The Paris fashion industry and French perfume are world-famous. Aircraft industry mainly concentrated in the south – especially Toulouse, where Concorde was built in co-operation with the UK.
Tourism: An important money-earner for France. The Mediterranean coast is popular at all seasons. The high mountains, the Alps and Pyrenees, are good for skiing in winter and for walking in summer. The Atlantic coast and Brittany are popular in summer.

Paris has more tourists than any other city in the world. Its attractions include the Eiffel tower, Notre-Dame Cathedral, Montmartre, and the art collection in the Louvre.

Spain and Portugal

Spain and Portugal share an almost square *peninsula*, called the Iberian Peninsula, which is cut off from the rest of Europe by the high Pyrenees. These mountains are difficult to cross, and most traffic uses routes along the Atlantic or Mediterranean coasts. The central part of the peninsula is a high plateau called the Meseta. It is divided by mountain ridges and deep valleys. The Meseta is very hot in summer, but can be bitterly cold in winter. The highest mountains are in the Sierra Nevada – a range which forms an attractive background to the Mediterranean coast.

Around most of Spain, the mountains and hills sweep down to the coast which has many cliffs and sandy bays. Portugal has a wide coastal plain with dunes and lagoons in the far south.

SPAIN	PORTUGAL
Area: 504,782 sq km	**Area:** 92,082 sq km (including Azores and Madeira)
Population: 38, 671,000	**Population:** 10,390,000
Capital (population): Madrid (3,146,000)	**Capital (population):** Lisbon (1,034,000)
Highest point: Mulhacén, 3478 m (Sierra Nevada)	**Highest point:** Estrêla, 1991 m
Official language: Spanish	**Official language:** Portuguese
Currency: Peseta	**Currency:** Escudo
Main exports: Manufactured goods, textiles, chemicals, leather goods, wine, fruit, fish, olive oil, vegetables, other foods	**Main exports:** Timber and wood products (including cork), textiles, machinery, wine, chemicals, sardines

Spain

Andorra

Portugal

SEEKING THE SUN

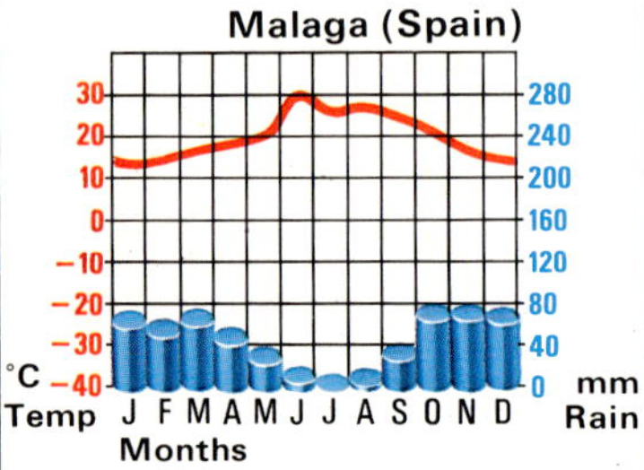

Weather: On the Mediterranean coast of Spain and in the south of Portugal, summers are hot and dry with lots of sunshine. Most rain comes in winter – but there is plenty of sunshine for holidaymakers throughout the year. Inland, it is drier with very hot summers. The Atlantic coasts are cooler with rain all year.

Tourism: Holiday resorts are found on all coasts, with big hotels and apartment blocks. New ones are being developed and this benefits the building industry, transport, craftwork and market-gardening. Main resort areas are: Costa Brava (north of Barcelona), Costa Blanca (near Valencia), Costa del Sol (near Malaga), the Algarve (southern Portugal), the Balearic Islands (especially Majorca), and the Canary Islands (off North Africa).

Other attractions: Mountain scenery in Pyrenees and Sierra Nevada; volcanoes on Canary Islands; historic sites such as Granada dating from Arab occupation of southern Spain, and the palaces, cathedrals and other fine buildings from the days when Spain and Portugal were great trading nations.

FARMING AND INDUSTRY

Farming: Very important in both countries for employment and exports. Spain is the world's leading producer of olives which grow everywhere on drier land. Olive oil is used for fish canning in Portugal. Vines grown on Mediterranean coast and in main valleys for wine-making – sherry comes from Cadiz and port from Oporto. Some grapes are used for dried fruit. Citrus fruit is important, especially on the Mediterranean coast: oranges are a major Spanish export. Cereals such as wheat and barley are the main crops on the central plateau. Sheep and goats are grazed in the south, cattle in the north.

Forests: Cork oak especially important in Portugal.

Fishing: Portugal's chief industry – mainly sardines, anchovy, tunny (tuna).

Industry: Being developed in both countries, mainly near large towns. Heavy industry in north Spain.

MINI-STATES

ANDORRA
Area: 453 sq km
Population: 32,700
Capital (population): Andorra la Vella (12,000)
Official language: Catalan
A small state high in the Pyrenees. Most people live in valley of River Valira. Often cut off in winter when road to France and Spain blocked by snow. Attracts visitors through tax-free shops, skiing and summer sports. Main income comes from tourism and the sale of stamps.

GIBRALTAR
Area: 6 sq km
Population: 31,000
Official language: English
A British *colony*, claimed by Spain. The land frontier between the two was reopened in 1983. Gibraltar, a limestone block jutting out into the Mediterranean, is strategically important as it guards the narrow Straits of Gibraltar. The naval base and tourist industry employ most people.

GREAT EMPIRES

Spain and Portugal once had large empires. Five hundred years ago explorers set sail from their coasts and discovered and conquered large parts of the Americas, Asia and Africa. Spain ruled most of South and Central America, parts of North America, parts of North Africa, and the Philippines in Asia. Portugal ruled Brazil, large areas of West and Southern Africa and small parts of South-East Asia.

Spain and Portugal led the world in the 16th century. Then came a long decline in power and importance. Spain lost most of her Empire in the 1820s; Portugal kept many colonies until recently.

◀ **Portugal:** fishermen mend their nets by the Atlantic Ocean.

▼ **Spain:** almond trees on the hills behind a new holiday resort.

Italy and its Neighbours

Italy

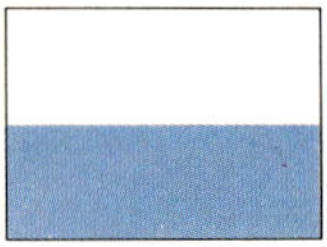
San Marino

Vatican City

Malta

Italy is a *peninsula* 1220 kilometres long which sticks out into the Mediterranean Sea like a boot. Sicily, Sardinia and many smaller islands are also part of Italy. Much of the country is mountainous. Between the Alps in the north and the Apennines is the broad Po valley with the richest farmland and the main industrial areas.

Southern Italy and the islands are poorer regions. Here, much of the land is steep, soil is thin and water is scarce. *Earthquakes* cause damage, and there are several active volcanoes. Many people have emigrated from the south to northern Italy and overseas.

Vatican City State and San Marino are two independent countries entirely within Italy. The Republic of Malta consists of two islands, Malta and Gozo, in the Mediterranean Sea. Ancient temples found here are among the oldest buildings known.

FACTS AND FIGURES

ITALY
Area: 301,252 sq km
Population: 56,189,000
Capital (population): Rome (3,700,000)
Highest point: Monte Bianco (Mont Blanc) 4810 m
Official language: Italian
Currency: Lira
Main exports: Machinery, motor vehicles, iron and steel, textiles, footwear, plastics, fruit

SAN MARINO
Area: 61 sq km
Population: 21,000
Capital (population): San Marino (4000)
Highest point: Mt Titano, 739 m
Official language: Italian
Currency: Italian lira
Income: Mainly from tourists and postage stamps

VATICAN CITY STATE
Area: 0·44 sq km (44 hectares) – the world's smallest independent state
Population: 1000
Governed by the Roman Catholic Church, with the Pope as Head of State.
Official languages: Italian, Latin
Currency: Italian lira

MALTA
Area: 316 sq km
Population: 340,000
Capital (population): Valletta (14,000)
Official languages: Maltese, English
Highest point: 249 m
Currency: Maltese pound
Main exports: Manufactured goods, food, ship repairing and tourism very important

WEST GERMANY
AUSTRIA
SWITZERLAND
FRANCE
YUGOSLAVIA
ITALY
SAN MARINO
VATICAN CITY STATE
CORSICA (France)
SARDINIA (Italy)
SICILY
MALTA
Kilometres
0 50 100 150 200 250
0 50 100 150
Miles
N
Matterhorn 4478 m
4810 m
4634 m
4061 m
4094 m
Lake Como
Lake Garda
Brescia
Milan
Verona
Padua
Venice
Trieste
Turin
Po
3841 m
Parma
Modena
Ferrara
Bologna
Genoa
3297 m
2165 m
Rimini
Florence
Pisa
Livorno
Ancona
Siena
Apennines
Assisi
2478 m
Tiber
2914 m
Rome
LIGURIAN SEA
ADRIATIC SEA
2710 m
Ajaccio
Sassari
1834 m
Cagliari
Bari
Naples
1277 m Mt Vesuvius
Salerno
Capri
Taranto
Brindisi
TYRRHENIAN SEA
Stromboli
Vulcano
Messina
Reggio
Palermo
3340 m Mt Etna
Catania
MEDITERRANEAN SEA
Valetta

THE LAND

Mountains: The Alps in the north have the highest mountains and the most spectacular scenery (Monte Bianco, 4810 m and Monte Rosa, 4638 m). The Apennines stretch down the centre of the country (Monte Corno 2914 m). *Volcanoes* include Vesuvius (near Naples); Etna (Sicily); Stromboli and Volcano (Lipari Islands).
Rivers: Longest is the Po (650 km). Others include the Tiber and the Arno.
Lakes: Several beautiful lakes in Alps: Maggiore, Como and Garda. Lake Trasimeno in the Apennines.
Islands: Sicily (25,707 sq km) and Sardinia (24,089 sq km); many smaller islands and groups of islands.

REGIONS OF ITALY

Region	Capital
Abruzzi	Aquila
Apulia	Bari
Basilicata	Potenza
Calabria	Catanzaro
Campania	Naples
Emilia – Romagna	Bologna
Friuli – Venezia Giulia	Trieste
Latium	Rome
Liguria	Genoa
Lombardy	Milan
Marche	Ancona
Molise	Campobasso
Piedmont	Turin
Sardinia	Cagliari
Sicily	Palermo
Tretino – Alto Adige	Trento
Tuscany	Florence
Umbria	Perugia
Valle d'Aosta	Aosta
Veneto	Venice

▼ **Italy** has several volcanoes near its coastline. Cereal crops grow on the flatter land. Olives, vines and fruit trees grow on the hill slopes.

ITALY FOR TOURISTS

People have been on tours to Italy for several hundred years.
Weather: The Alps and the Po Valley have cold winters; the rest of Italy has a *Mediterranean climate* with mild winters and hot, dry summers.
Historic cities: Rome and cities in north Italy, such as Florence, Verona and Bologna. Venice is unique: transport is by canal in the old town, and gondolas and motor boats called vaporetti are used to ferry people to and fro. Other areas have superb Roman ruins.
Holiday resorts: Beaches on the Adriatic coast and the islands of Capri and Elba are popular with holidaymakers. Sicily has fine beaches, ancient Greek temples and an active volcano to climb. Other resorts include many in the Alps – for skiing in winter and sailing on the lakes in summer.

FARMING AND INDUSTRY

Farming: 60% of the land is farmed – the rest is too mountainous. Marshes have been drained. About 7% of those working are employed in farming.
Main crops: Wheat (for bread and pasta), vines for wine, maize, citrus fruit, olives.
Livestock: Cattle kept in north; sheep and goats in hilly areas of south.
Energy: Mainly from *hydro-electric* power in the north, natural gas in the south. Coal and oil are imported.
Industry: Mainly in the north, but the government is encouraging factories to move to poorer south.
Important industries: Vehicles (Fiat in Turin; Lancia and Alfa Romeo cars; Lambretta and Vespa scooters; Pirelli tyres); typewriters (Olivetti); refrigerators, washing machines and many other electrical goods; textiles; printing (this book was printed in Milan); food processing, such as canned tomatoes, pasta and olive oil.

Poland, Czechoslovakia & Hungary

Poland and Hungary are countries with plenty of flat land, and between them lies mountainous Czechoslovakia. Much of this small country is occupied by the forested Carpathian Mountains which are highest in the High Tatras, on the Polish border. Time and again, the forests and valleys of Czechoslovakia have inspired beautiful music and exciting stories.

Poland is the only country of the three with a coast. Inland from the coastal dunes and lagoons there is flat land which is part of the North European Plain. Much of this area is infertile, with lots of heath, marsh and lakes. The land is richer in the south where the main towns, such as Warsaw and Lodz are found. Poland's mineral and industrial areas are further south, although shipbuilding is important at the Baltic port of Gdansk in the north.

South of the Carpathians stretches the Hungarian plain, crossed by the river Danube. The landscape is flat and monotonous but makes good farmland. Lake Balaton is Europe's largest freshwater lake.

Polish, Czech and Slovak are Slavic languages. Czech is spoken in the west of Czechoslovakia, Slovak in the east. Hungarian is a totally different language: like Finnish, it originated in Central Asia. The people and language are sometimes called Magyar.

▼ **Poland**: Warsaw's market-place was rebuilt in its old style after wartime bombing.

0 50 100 150 200 Kilometres
0 50 100 Miles
N
BALTIC SEA
USSR
Gdansk
Szczecin
Bydgoszcz
Netze
Oder
Vistula
Bug
Poznan
Warta
Warsaw
EAST
ERMANY
Neisse
POLAND
Lodz
Wroclaw
Lublin
Katowice
Krakow
Prague
Elbe
1492
Plzen
Ostrava
USSR
CZECHOSLOVAKIA
Carpathian Mts
Brno
Vltava
Vah
2655
WEST
ERMANY
Kosice
Bratislava
Miskolc
Danube
AUSTRIA
Budapest
Debrecen
Tisza
Lake Balaton
HUNGARY
ITALY
ROMANIA
Szeged
Pecs
YUGOSLAVIA
DRIATIC
SEA

FACTS AND FIGURES

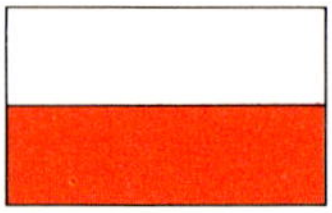
Poland

Czechoslovakia

Hungary

POLAND
Area: 312,677 sq km
Population: 36,300,000
Capital (population): Warsaw (1,572,000)
Highest point: Rysy Peak, 2503 m
Official language: Polish
Currency: Zloty
Main exports: Coal, lignite, coke, iron and steel, ships, vehicles, textiles, food

CZECHOSLOVAKIA
Area: 127,869 sq km
Population: 15,556,000
Capital (population): Prague (1,189,000)
Highest point: Gerlachovsky, 2655 m
Official languages: Czech, Slovak
Currency: Koruna
Main exports: Machinery, other manufactured goods, raw materials and fuels

HUNGARY
Area: 93,030 sq km
Population: 10,850,00
Capital (population): Budapest (2,093,000)
Highest point: Mt Kekes, 1015 m
Official language: Hungarian
Currency: Forint
Main exports: Transport equipment, electrical goods, bauxite and aluminium, food, pharmaceuticals, wine

FARMING AND INDUSTRY

Farming: This is important in each country, occupying 65–75% of the land. Almost all the farms in Hungary and Czechoslovakia are run as State or Collective farms. In Poland a lot of the land is still in small privately owned farms.
Main crops: Arable farming is the most important. Oats, rye and potatoes are main crops on poorer soils (northern Poland, hills of Czechoslovakia); wheat, barley and sugar beet on fertile lowlands. Hungary and Czechoslovakia have hotter summers so maize, sunflowers and tobacco are grown. Vineyards and orchards on south-facing slopes.
Industry: Increasing in all these countries: imports from the USSR add to local resources.
Energy: Coal (Poland is major producer; some across the border in Czechoslovakia); brown coal; gas (Poland), and some *hydro-electric power.*
Other minerals: Sulphur, lead, nickel and copper (Poland); iron ore (Czechoslovakia, with some low-quality ores in Poland); bauxite (Hungary) and other minerals.
Major industries: Iron and steel industry, with related engineering, is found in all countries. Poland produces a vast range of manufactured goods from ships to shoes. Budapest has Europe's largest bus factory; Czechoslovakia is the home of Bata shoes. Chemicals, textiles and food processing are also important industries.

◀ **Hungary:** Buda and Pest are separated by the Danube. Many barges use this river.

CAPITAL CITIES

In each country, the capital city is by far the largest and most important.
Warsaw began as a port on the River Vistula 700 years ago. It was almost destroyed in World War II but has been rebuilt. Many historic parts have been rebuilt to look exactly as they did in the past.
Prague (Praha) is the capital of the Czech part of Czechoslovakia and of the whole country. The Slovak capital is Bratislava, an important port on the Danube.
Budapest was two separate towns 100 years ago. Buda is built on hills west of the River Danube; Pest on low land on the east bank. Now they are one town linked by eight bridges. Three-quarters of Hungary's factories and a fifth of the population are in Budapest.

RECENT HISTORY

These three countries won their freedom in 1918, after World War I. Before then, Poland had been divided between Prussia (part of Germany), Austria and Russia; Czechoslovakia and Hungary had been part of the great Austrian Empire.

In World War II, these countries were occupied by Germany. In 1943–1945 the USSR advanced from the East to drive out the Germans. Since then, these countries have had Communist governments allied to the USSR.

The Balkans and Romania

These five countries are all mountainous. The mountains are beautiful, but they are difficult to cross, and they separate different groups of people speaking different languages. The forested Carpathians in Romania are said to be the home of the fictional Count Dracula. South of the broad Danube valley are the mainly limestone hills of the Balkan *peninsula*. Summers are hot and dry, and water sinks into the ground easily, so the mountains are arid and only useful as grazing land for sheep and goats. The best farmland is the low land near the Danube. This mighty river flows into the Black Sea through Europe's largest *delta*.

The Black Sea coast of Romania and Bulgaria is flat, with long sandy beaches and many holiday resorts. The Adriatic coastline of Yugoslavia, Albania and Greece is quite different – very rugged, but very beautiful. The Aegean Sea is dotted with thousands of Greek islands and divided by many narrow peninsulas. The sunny weather, the scenery, and the fascinating ruins attract many tourists to Greece and Yugoslavia. Albania, however, remains a mysterious country which has little contact with the rest of Europe.

USSR
Carpathian Mts
Iasi
Cluj
Timisoara
Brasov
Tisa
2543
Transylvania Alps
2518m
Galati
i Sad
Turnu Severin
Ploesti
ROMANIA
Belgrade
Craiova
Bucharest
Constanta
Morava
Danube
Ruse
Iskar
BLACK SEA
Nis
BULGARIA
Varna
22m
Sofia
Balkan Mts
Burgas
2496m
2692m
Mt Musala 2925
Maritsa
Shkoder
Skopje
Plovdiv
Rhodope Mts
2762m
Vardar
Tirane
2480m
Thessaloniki
ALBANIA
2637m
Pindus Mts
Mt Olympus
2917
AEGEAN SEA
GREECE
TURKEY
Delphi
Athens
Piraeus
2376
Olympia
ONIAN SEA
NAXOS
Sparti
RHODES
MEDITERRANEAN SEA
CRETE
Iraklion

Country (language)	Area (in sq km)	Population	Capital (population)	Highest point
ALBANIA (Albanian)	28,748	2,873,000	Tirane (198,000)	Mt Korabi, 2762 m
BULGARIA (Bulgarian)	110,912	8,990,000	Sofia (1,032,000)	Musala, 2925 m
GREECE (Greek)	131,994	9,665,000	Athens (2,540,000)	Mt Olympus, 2917 m
ROMANIA (Romanian)	237,500	22,653,000	Bucharest (1,960,000)	Negoiu, 2543 m
YUGOSLAVIA (Serbo-Croat, Slovene, Macedonian)	255,804	22,745,000	Belgrade (1,209,000)	Triglav, 2865m

◀ **Yugoslavia:** holiday-makers at a resort on the beautiful Adriatic coast.

Currency	Main exports
Lek	Metals (chrome, nickel, copper), oil, bitumen, tobacco, fruit and vegetables
Lev	Machinery, metals, food, tobacco, textiles
Drachma	Manufactured goods, food, animals, wine, tobacco, chemicals
Leu	Machinery, minerals, metals, oil, natural gas, food, chemicals
Dinar	Machinery, electrical goods transport equipment, chemicals

▼ **Romania:** an old Christian monastery in the forested Carpathian mountains.

FARMING AND INDUSTRY

Farming: Important in all these countries. Bulgaria has the highest proportion of arable land. Although winters are cold in the north, summers are hot and sunny. Near the Mediterranean, rainfall is low and comes in winter. Higher land provides grazing for sheep and goats.
Major crops: Wheat, maize, barley, sugar beet, sunflowers, fruit (such as plums in Bulgaria, citrus fruit in Greece), vines (grapes for sultanas in Greece), tobacco, cotton.
Minerals: Oil very important in Romania. Small amounts of minerals in mountains (lead, bauxite, copper), marble in Greece.
Industry: Based on local raw materials. Many food-processing industries (such as jam and canned fruit from Bulgaria; olive oil and dried fruit from Greece). Fishing and shipping important in Greece.
Tourism: Very important in Greece and Yugoslavia.

LANGUAGES

Romanian: Written in Latin letters, has many Latin words.
Bulgarian: A Slavic language written in the Cyrillic alphabet (like Russian).
Greek: An ancient language with its own alphabet (the first letters are 'alpha' and 'beta').
Albanian: Some similarities with Greek, but is written in Latin letters.
Yugoslavia: Five main nationalities who use 3 different slavic languages: Serbo-Croat, Macedonian and Slovenian. Both the Latin and Cyrillic alphabets are used.

USSR

The USSR is the largest country in the world and stretches across both Europe and Asia. USSR stands for Union of Soviet Socialist Republics, and 15 Republics make up the Union. Three-quarters of the country is the Russian Soviet Federal Socialist Republic (the RSFSR) which includes most of European USSR and Siberia. Russian is the language of the capital, and of more than half of the people of the whole country, so the USSR is often called Russia.

This country is as large as a continent. A train journey from Leningrad on the Baltic Sea to Vladivostok on the Sea of Japan takes

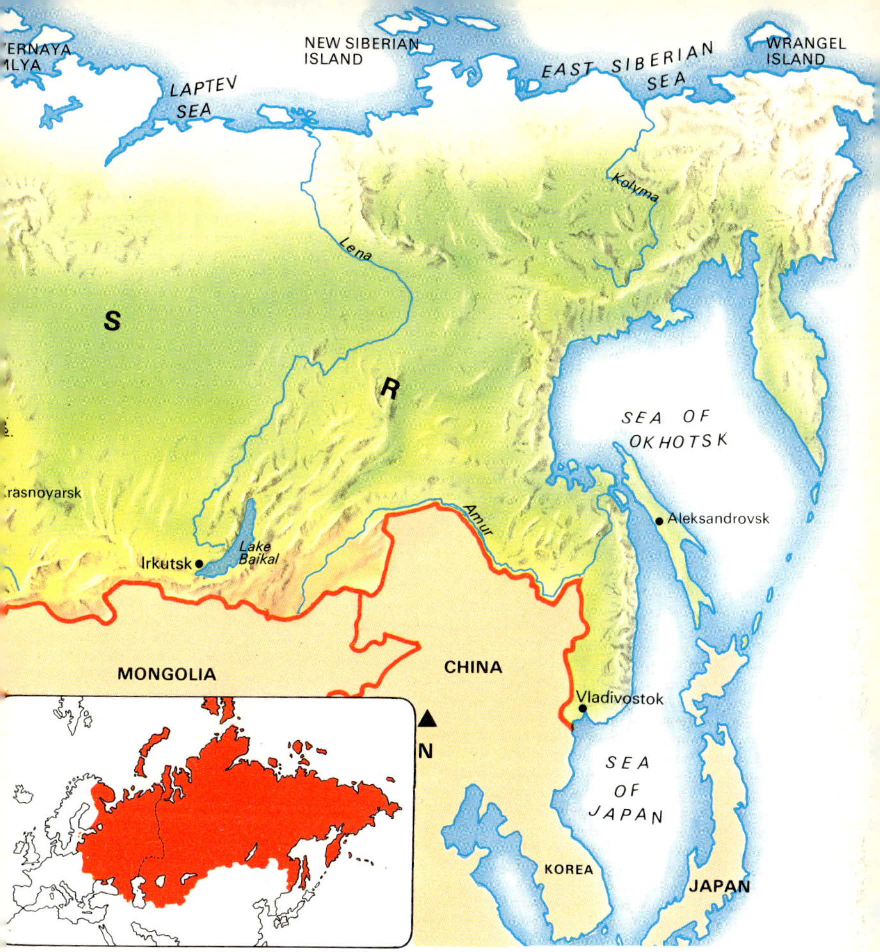

eight days and, during the journey, passengers have to put their watches forward by an hour seven times as they cross into new time zones.

Within its borders, the USSR has a great variety of climate and scenery from Arctic wastes, endless coniferous forests and grassy *plains* to *deserts* and high mountains. Many different crops can be grown and a large number of minerals are mined and used as the raw materials for a great variety of industry.

The USSR has a Communist government. The flag shows two symbols of work: the hammer, for industry, and the sickle, for farming (sickles were used for harvesting crops). Together, they symbolize a country that is run by the workers: a key idea of Communism.

FACTS AND FIGURES

Official name: Soyuz Sovyetschikh Sotsialisticheskikh Respublik
Area: 22,402,200 sq km (European USSR, west of Urals: 5,571,000 sq km)
Population: 268,800,000
Capital (population): Moscow (8,099,000)
Highest point: Communism Peak, 7495 m, in the Pamir Mts
Official language: Russian
Currency: Rouble
Longest river: Yenisei (5540 km) is 4th longest river in the world
Largest lake: Caspian Sea (438,695 sq km) is the world's largest lake
Lowest point: Bed of Lake Baikal (1484 m below sea level). This is the world's deepest lake

INDUSTRY

This has expanded dramatically in 60 years.
Energy: Plenty of coal, oil, gas and *hydro-electric power.*
Minerals: Huge iron ore deposits supply iron and steel industry and many engineering industries. Many other minerals are worked including silver, gold, diamonds, asbestos, manganese, phosphates, potash, copper, zinc and bauxite.
Chief industries: Iron and steel industries (USSR is a top world producer); chemical industry; timber and paper from wood – forests cover 40% of the land; textiles (especially cotton) and food processing using raw materials from fishing and farming; other manufactured products including consumer goods.
Industrial areas: Ukraine, southern Urals, Moscow, Gorki and Leningrad. Small centres are developing in south and east.

▼ **Wheat is harvested** by combines on a huge state farm in the Steppes.

CLIMATE

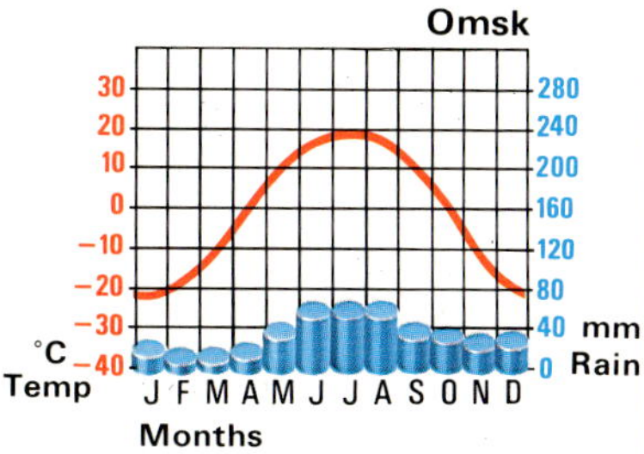

Moscow and Omsk are on almost the same line of latitude. But Omsk is further east, in Siberia, and far from any sea. So Omsk has only half as much rain and snow as Moscow.

Summer temperatures are about the same, but compare the winter temperatures: Moscow may seem cold, but Omsk is far colder. Further east and north in Siberia it is even colder. Siberia is remote, with few people. But new towns are growing, and mineral finds are making the region more important.

Moscow and Omsk are further south than Bergen in Norway. But compare these graphs with the one on page 31.

▼ **A pipeline** is built through the Siberian forest to carry natural gas to European Russia.

FARMING

Only about 25% of the land is used for farming, 10% for crops and the rest for grazing animals. Most farmland is in European USSR. Farms are either huge state farms ('sovkhoz' – average size 60 sq km) or collective farms ('kolkhoz' – average size 30 sq km). A collective farm has a group of families co-operating in the work and sharing the profits. Each family also has a small plot of land for fruit and vegetables.

Main crops: Cereals, especially on the rich black soils of the steppe (once grassland areas). But harvests are sometimes poor and grain is imported. Sugar beet, root vegetables, sunflowers, cotton also important. In the far south: tea, tobacco, fruit, grapes. Irrigation is necessary in desert areas.

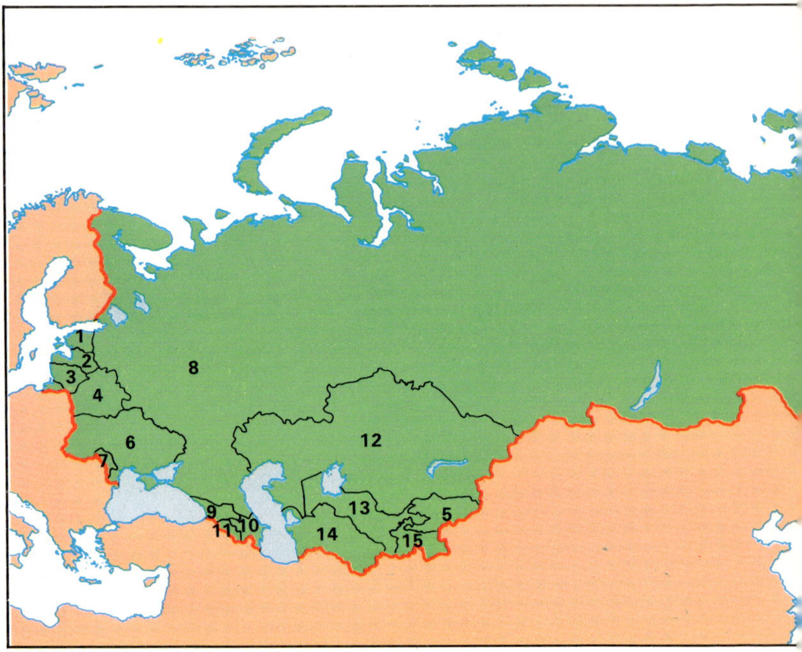
1
2
3
4
5
6
7
8
9
10
11
12
13
14
15

REPUBLICS OF THE USSR

Republic (Capital)	Area (in sq km)	Population
11 Armenia (Yerevan)	29,800	3,100,000
10 Azerbaijan (Baku)	86,600	6,200,000
3 Byelorussia (Minsk)	207,600	9,600,000
1 Estonia (Tallinn)	45,100	1,500,000
9 Georgia (Tbilisi)	69,700	5,000,000
12 Kazakhastan (Alma-Ata)	2,717,300	15,900,000
5 Kirgizia (Frunze)	198,500	3,600,000
2 Latvia (Riga)	63,700	2,500,000
4 Lithuania (Vilnius)	65,200	3,400,000
7 Moldavia (Kishinev)	33,700	4,000,000
8 Russian SFSR (Moscow)	17,075,400	139,400,000
15 Tadzhikistan (Dushanbe)	143,100	4,000,000
14 Turkmenistan (Ashkhabad)	488,100	3,000,000
6 Ukraine (Kiev)	603,700	50,000,000
13 Uzbekistan (Tashkent)	447,400	15,800,000

PEOPLES AND LANGUAGES

The USSR has a great variety of peoples: each republic is the home of a major ethnic group (a group of people who share the same traditions, culture or language). Most people live in the European USSR. Russians are the biggest single group, but there are many other people with their own languages, for example Latvians, Lithuanians and Estonians. The Ukraine has the highest average density of population.

The Asiatic part of the USSR has a very low population density – an average of only 2 per square kilometre and much of the north is also empty. But the population increase is higher than in Europe. In the south, many people are Muslims.

More than 60 languages are spoken in the USSR, but everyone has to learn Russian at school. Russian is written in the Cyrillic alphabet. Centuries ago, St Cyril based this alphabet partly on Latin letters and partly on Greek. CCCP on stamps and coins represents SSSR: the initials of the country in Russian.

The ten largest ethnic groups are: Russians (52·2%), Ukrainians (16%), Uzbeks (4·8%), Byelorussians (3·6%), Kazakhs (2·5%), Tartars (2·4%), Azerbaijanians (2%), Armenians (1·6%), Georgians (1·4%) and Moldavians (1·1%).

◀ **Red Square** is in the centre of Moscow.

Asia

Asia is the world's largest continent. It stretches for over 7500 kilometres from the Mediterranean to the Pacific Ocean, and for about 6500 kilometres from the shores of the Arctic Ocean to the islands of Indonesia.

More than half the world's people live in Asia, yet vast stretches are almost uninhabited. Northern Asia is in the USSR, where winters are long and cold. Central Asia is *desert*, from the hot deserts of Arabia to the inland Gobi with its harsh winters. And much of Asia is mountainous. The Himalayas have the world's highest peaks, and other ranges stretch through Central Asia and into the *peninsulas* of the South-East. Much of the mainland and many of the islands of

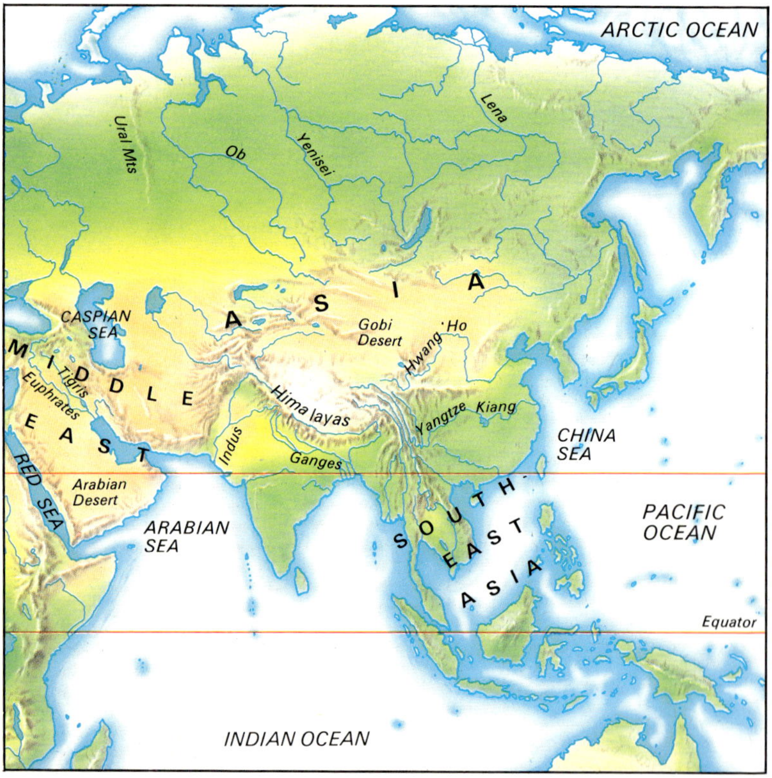

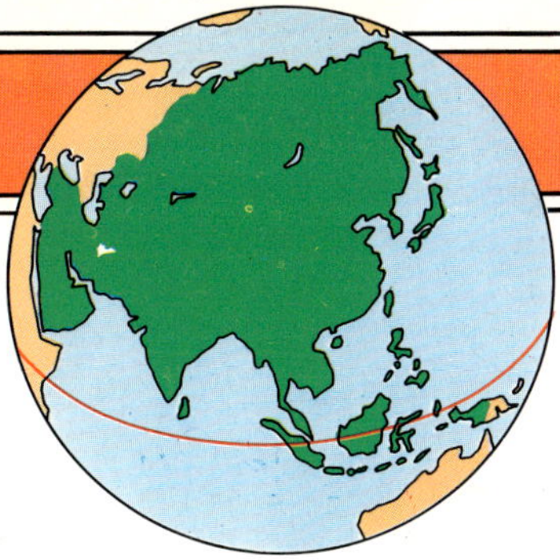

tropical Asia are covered in thick forest and have very heavy rainfall for part of the year.

Areas which have good soil and sufficient rain for growing crops are very crowded indeed. Besides densely populated rural areas, Asia has more large cities than any other continent – and the world's largest city, Tokyo, is in Japan.

AREA:
44,387,000 sq km (including USSR east of the Urals and Turkey in Asia).
POPULATION:
2,693,000,000
INDEPENDENT COUNTRIES: 41
HIGHEST POINT:
Mt Everest (8848 m) world's highest peak.
LOWEST POINT:
Shore of the Dead Sea (393 m below sea level), the world's lowest point.
LARGEST LAKE:
Caspian Sea (438,695 sq km).
LONGEST RIVERS:
Yenisei (5540 km), Yangtze (5530 km), Ob (5410 km), Hwang Ho (4830 km).

RICHEST COUNTRIES
(GNP per person – see p. 19: United Arab Emirates ($30,070), Qatar ($26,080), Kuwait ($22,840). Japan has a GNP of $9890 per person.
POOREST COUNTRIES:
Bhutan ($80), Bangladesh ($120), Nepal ($140).

▲ **Iran:** an ancient mosque in Esfahan.

▼ **Thailand:** many kinds of fruit and vegetables are sold from boats at the floating market on the waterways of Bangkok.

China and its Neighbours

Amur
MANCHURIA
Ulan Bator
OLIA
Harbin
Hsi-Liao
Shenyang
Fushun
Anshan
NORTH KOREA
ER MONGOLIA
Huhhot
Hwang Ho
Beijing (Peking)
Tangshan
Tianjin (Tientsin)
Pyongyang
Seoul
SOUTH KOREA
Yinchuan
Taiyuan
Shijiazhuang
Jinan (Tsinan)
Poshan
Pusan
anzhou
YELLOW SEA
Zhengzhou
Xian (Sian)
Nanjing
Hefei
Shanghai
Yangtze Kiang
Wuhan
Hangzhou
EAST CHINA SEA
Nanchang
Changsha
Fuzhou
Guiyang
Taipei
TAIWAN
Si-Kiang
Guangzhou (Canton)
Nanning
MACAO (Portugal)
HONG KONG (Britain)
PACIFIC OCEAN
VIETNAM
SOUTH CHINA SEA
HAINAN

China is the third largest country in the world but the first country to have more than a billion (a thousand million) people. But this population is very unevenly distributed. Vast areas of *desert* in the north-west are completely empty and few people live in the western three-quarters of the country. This part is mountainous – including the whole of the autonomous region of Tibet, a high bleak *plateau* with towering mountain peaks.

Ninety per cent of China's people live on fifteen per cent of the land in the eastern part of the country. In the lower parts of the great river valleys, every patch of fertile land is used. South of the River Yangtze it is hot for most of the year and rice is the main food crop. Further north, winters are cold and other cereals, such as wheat and barley, are grown.

Chinese people are proud of their long history, but for the majority of people life has always been hard. Floods, famines and *earthquakes* have been common. Since 1949, China has had a Communist government. People are organized into communes, responsible for farms, factories and welfare. Farming is being improved and new land is being cultivated. Minerals are being exploited, industry is growing in importance, and transport and housing are improving.

Country	Area (in sq km)	Population	Capital (population)
CHINA	9,596,961	1,008,176,000	Peking (Beijing) (8,706,000)
HONG KONG	1045	4,957,000	Victoria (767,000)
MACAO	16	333,000	Macao (157,000)
MONGOLIA	1,565,000	1,772,000	Ulan Bator (400,000)
NORTH KOREA	120,538	18,908,000	Pyongyang (1,500,000)
SOUTH KOREA	98,484	39,546,000	Seoul (8,367,000)
TAIWAN (formerly Formosa)	35,961	17,100,000	Taipei (3,050,000)

▲ **China:** rush hour in Xian (Sian), capital of Shaanxi Province.

▲ **Hong Kong:** a busy shopping street filled with cars.

Government	Official language	Currency	Main exports
Communist republic	Chinese (Mandarin)	Yuan	Industrial and agricultural products
British colony	English, Chinese (Cantonese)	HK dollar	Light manu-factured goods
Portuguese colony	Portuguese, Chinese	Pataca	Light manu-factured goods
Communist republic	Mongol	Tugrik	Cattle, horses, wool, hair
Communist republic	Korean	Won	Iron and other metal ores
Republic	Korean	Won	Textiles, manu-factured goods, chemicals
Republic	Chinese (Mandarin)	Taiwan dollar	Textiles, electrical goods, food, machinery, plastics

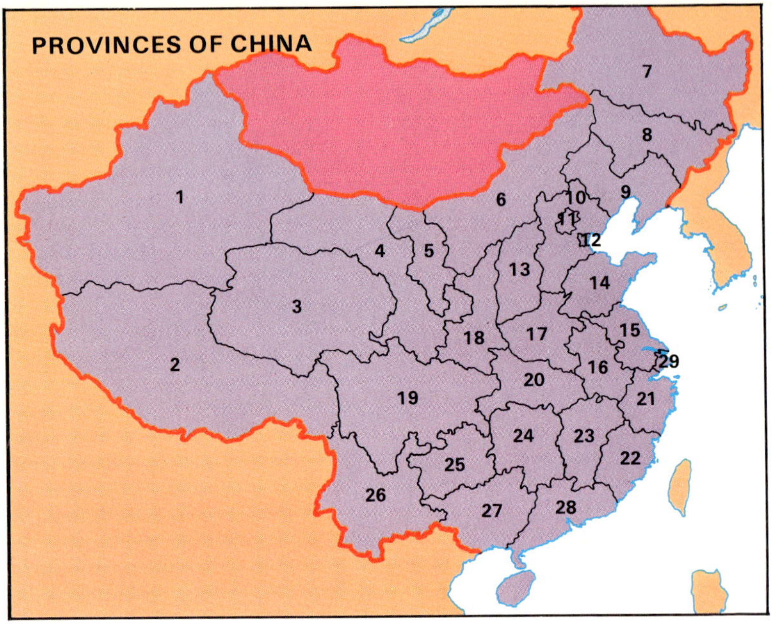

CHINA'S NEIGHBOURS

TAIWAN:
A non-Communist Chinese republic, calling itself Nationalist China. It has been independent from the mainland since 1949.

HONG KONG: (a British colony); **MACAO** (a Portuguese colony)
Two of the most densely populated places in the world, with many high-rise buildings. Most people are Chinese – more have moved here from China since 1949.
These three small, crowded countries have developed industries and export a great range of small consumer goods. Service industries like tourism, shipping, banking, and import and export arrangements for other countries are important.

MONGOLIA:
A *desert* country with close links with the USSR. It was once the centre of a vast empire stretching from Japan to Hungary and including most of China and the USSR. Mongolia is the world's largest land-locked country but one of the least populated. Animal herding is still the main activity.

KOREA:
Since the war of 1953, North Korea has been a Communist country independent of South Korea. Both countries are rich in minerals. Industry has developed rapidly, and farming has been improved and mechanised. North Korea has developed with the help of the USSR, while South Korea has received American aid.

PROVINCES OF CHINA

Province (*old name)	Area (sq km)	Population	Capital (*old name)
16 Anhui (Anhwei)	139,900	48,000,000	Hefei (Hofei)
22 Fujian (Fukien)	123,100	24,000,000	Fuzhou (Foochow)
4 Gansu (Kansu)	530,000	22,000,000	Lanzhou (Lanchow)
28 Guangdong (Kwangtung)	231,400	55,000,000	Guangzhou (Canton)
25 Guizhou (Kweichow)	174,000	26,000,000	Guiyang (Kweiyang)
10 Hebei (Hopei)	202,700	52,000,000	Shijiazhuang
7 Heilongjiang (Heilungkiang)	710,000	*33,000,000	Harbin
17 Henan (Honan)	167,000	73,000,000	Zhengzhou (Chengel)
20 Hubei (Hupei)	187,500	45,000,000	Wuhan
24 Hunan (Hunan)	210,500	51,000,000	Changsha
15 Jiangsu (Kiangsu)	102,200	58,000,000	Nanjing (Nanking)
23 Jiangxi (Kiangsi)	164,800	31,000,000	Nanchang
8 Jilin (Kirin)	290,000	24,000,000	Changchun
9 Liaoning (Liaoning)	230,000	37,000,000	Shenyang
3 Qinghai (Tsinghai)	721,000	5,000,000	Xining (Sining)
18 Shaanxi (Shensi)	195,800	27,000,000	Xian (Sian)
14 Shandong (Shantung)	153,300	74,000,000	Jinan (Tsinan)
13 Shanxi (Shansi)	157,100	24,000,000	Taiyuan
19 Sichuan (Szechwan)	569,000	109,000,000	Chengdu (Chengtu)
26 Yunnan (Yunnan)	436,200	36,000,000	Kunming
21 Zhejiang (Chekiang)	101,800	39,000,000	Hangzhou (Hangchow)
Autonomous Region:			
27 Guangxi Zhuang (Kwangsi-Chuang)	220,400	34,000,000	Nanning
6 Nei Monggol (Inner Mongolia)	450,000	18,000,000	Huhhot (Huhehot)
5 Ningxia Hui (Ningsia-Hui)	170,000	4,000,000	Yinchuan (Yinchwan)
2 Tibet (Tibet)	1,121,600	3,000,000	Lhasa
1 Xinjiang Uygur (Sinkiang-Uigur)	1,646,800	12,000,000	Urunqi (Urumchi)
Municipality:			
11 Beijing (Peking)	17,800	10,000,000	
29 Shanghai (Shanghai)	5,800	13,000,000	
12 Tianjin (Tientsin)	4,000	10,000,000	

*Names are spelt differently because the Wades-Giles system of transliteration from Chinese to the Latin alphabet is being replaced by the Hanyupinyin system used in China. Children in China now learn to write in Hanyupinyin (using the Latin alphabet) before they learn Chinese characters. But sounds for letters in Hanyupinyin are different from English.

China

Mongolia

North Korea

South Korea

Japan

Japan is made up of four main islands and several thousand smaller ones. Most of the land is very mountainous, and every piece of flat land is valuable. There are over 160 *volcanoes*, of which 54 are still active. *Earthquakes* are common – fortunately, most cause little damage.

Japan has few raw materials of its own. It has to import most of those needed for its many industries, and some of its food. But since 1950 it has developed the skills of its large population to become the most prosperous and industrialized country in Asia. Today it is the world's largest producer of trucks, ships, televisions and radios.

FACTS AND FIGURES

Area: 372,313 sq km
Population: 120,055,000
Capital (population): Tokyo (11,695,000)
Highest point: Fujiyama, 3776 m
Official language: Japanese
Currency: Yen
Main exports: Chemicals, electronic goods, machinery, vehicles, optical equipment, ships, textiles

▼ **The 'Bullet Train'** runs between big cities and past small farms in the crowded countryside. In the background is Mt Fuji, a famous extinct volcano.

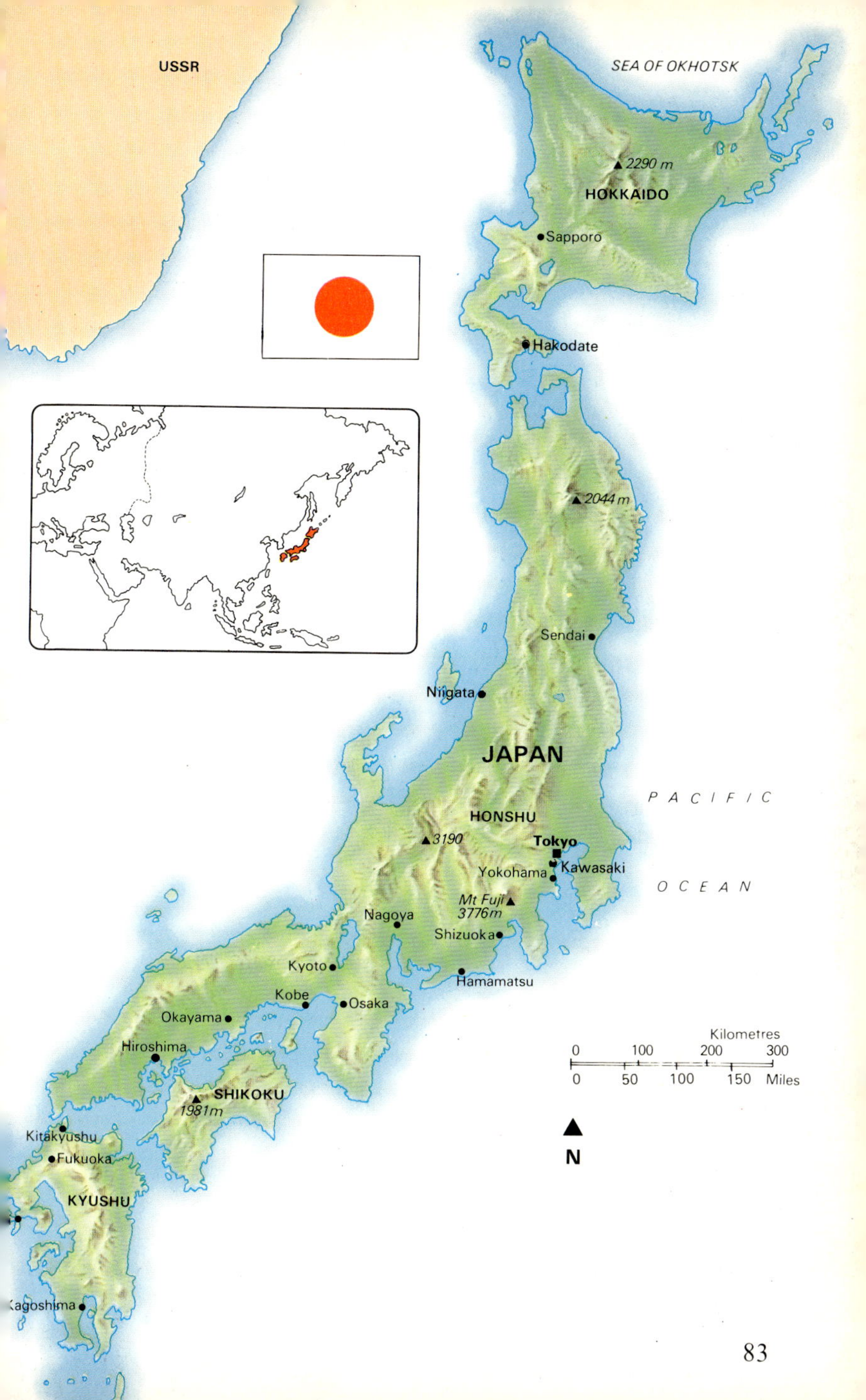
USSR
SEA OF OKHOTSK
2290 m
HOKKAIDO
Sapporo
Hakodate
2044 m
Sendai
Niigata
JAPAN
P A C I F I C
O C E A N
HONSHU
3190
Tokyo
Kawasaki
Yokohama
Mt Fuji
3776m
Nagoya
Shizuoka
Kyoto
Hamamatsu
Kobe
Osaka
Okayama
Hiroshima
SHIKOKU
1981m
Kitakyushu
Fukuoka
KYUSHU
Kagoshima
Kilometres
0 100 200 300
0 50 100 150 Miles
N

FARMING

Only 15% of the land area is used and farms are mostly small (average size 1 hectare). Hillsides are terraced to increase amount of flat land. Farmers are fewer in number now than in the past – only 13% of the working people – and the majority are part-timers or retired from other work.

Main crops: Rice (grown on half the arable land), fruit, vegetables, soya beans, barley and wheat.

Food production: Rice yields have more than doubled this century and there is now a rice surplus. But as people get richer they want a more varied diet, so food imports have increased.

Animals: Cattle and pigs.

Weather: Winters are very cold in the north, but frost is rare in the south. Summers are hot everywhere. *Monsoon* rains come May to September – heaviest in the south and east. Typhoons *(hurricanes)* are common.

INDUSTRY

Japan relies on importing raw materials from other countries bordering the Pacific. Its industrial methods are modern, with large, semi-automatic factories. Branches of Japanese factories have been set up in other countries, often to overcome trade restrictions – for example Japanese cars are made in 34 countries.

Main industries: Vehicles (cars, vans, motor-bikes, cycles) – now world's leading producer; electronic equipment (computers, calculators, office equipment, TVs, videos, industrial robots); iron and steel – has world's largest blast furnace; shipbuilding – has world's largest dry dock; consumer goods (cameras, watches); chemicals (fertilisers, plastics, fibres).

Pollution: A major problem as industry grew. Strict controls since 1971 have halved air pollution and improved water sufficiently for fish to return to bays near cities.

▲ **Elevated roads** and railways and high-rise buildings crowd central Tokyo.

◀ **The ice festival** in Hokkaido: northern Japan has very cold winters.

CITIES

Ten Japanese cities have over a million people each – 40% of the whole population. The total built-up area around Tokyo-Yokohama is the world's most populated urban area with nearly 30 million people.

Building land is scarce so high-rise buildings are common. Railways and roads are built one above another. Hills are being reshaped for more building land, and earth and rocks used to reclaim land from the sea. Kobe, for example, has two huge artificial islands built out of Mt Rokko. New developments have even been built underground – Osaka has an 80 hectare underground 'town'!

The five largest towns with their populations are:
Tokyo (8,349,000);
Yokohama (2,774,000);
Osaka (2,648,000);
Nagoya (2,088,000);
Kyoto (1,468,000).

THE BULLET TRAIN

This train was the first in the world to offer regular travel for passengers at over 200 kph. It uses special track – Shinkansen (new trunk line) – of standard gauge. There are two types of train: express – 'Hikari' (lightning) – and stopping – 'Kodama' (echo). The Tokyo-Osaka line, opened in 1964, is now extended to Hakata on Kyushu Island via an $18\frac{1}{2}$ km tunnel under the sea. The line north is being extended to Hokkaido via a 54 km tunnel – the world's longest railway tunnel. Lines are computer-operated and centrally controlled (even the automatic brakes). Trains have on-board telephones. Special problems include the mountainous land requiring many tunnels, bridges and viaducts, and frequent *earthquakes* – special detectors cut off power. Typhoon damage is common.

INDIA
CHINA
Mandalay
BURMA
3053 m
Irrawaddy
Salween
LAOS
Hanoi
Haiphong
Vientiane
THAILAND
Mekong
Rangoon
Chao Phraya
Hue
Da Nang
VIETNAM
ANDAMAN ISLANDS (India)
Bangkok
KAMPUCHEA (CAMBODIA)
Phnom-Penh
Ho Chi Minh City (Saigon)
GULF OF THAILAND
PALAWA
NICOBAR ISLANDS (India)
SOUTH CHINA SEA
4101
Penang
Bandar Seri Begawan
SABA
BRUNEI
MALAYSIA
Medan
Kuala Lumpur
SARAWAK
SINGAPORE
INDIAN OCEAN
Pontianak
SUMATRA
KALIMANTAN (BORNEO)
Padang
Palembang
Bandjarmasin
JAVA SEA
INDONESIA
Ujung Pand
N
Krakatoa
Jakarta
Bandung
Semarang
JAVA
Surabaja
SUMB
Surakarta
Malang
3676 m
BALI
Kilometres
0 200 400 600 800
0 100 200 300 400 500
Miles

South-East Asia

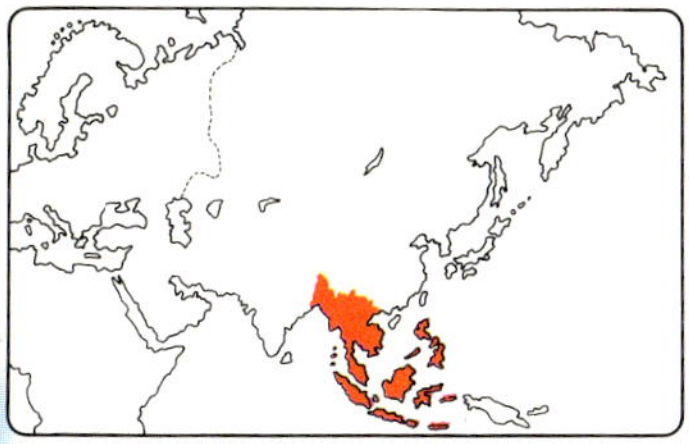

It is hot throughout the year in all of South-East Asia, and in most places the monsoon brings heavy rain for a few months. The *peninsulas* and islands which make up these countries are mostly mountainous, and some of the mountains are *volcanoes*. Thick *tropical* forests cover the mountainsides. In some countries they are being cut down and the valuable hardwoods, such as teak and mahogany, exported. In Burma, it is still a common sight to see elephants hauling tree trunks.

Many of the other exports of the area also come from trees, for example, rubber, copra (from coconuts), palm oil, bananas and spices. Such products mostly come from *plantations* planted when these countries were part of European empires.

Although the mountain areas are remote and thinly populated, most of the *plains* are very densely populated indeed. Java is not a big island, but more people live there than in any European country. Rice is the main food crop, and flooded terraces extend up many hillsides, tended with great care by farmers who may harvest several crops a year.

Mining is becoming more important as well as industry in the towns. Indonesia has oil, which is also the main export of the tiny Sultanate of Brunei. Tin, exported from Malaysia, is washed out of hillsides with huge jets of water.

Country (Independent)	Area (in sq km)	Population	Capital (population)
BRUNEI (1983)	5765	248,000	Bandar Seri Begawan (58,000)
BURMA (1948)	676,552	35,211,000	Rangoon (3,662,000)
INDONESIA (1949)	2,027,087	146,527,000	Djakarta (6,506,000)
KAMPUCHEA (1954)	181,035	8,559,000	Phnom Penh (2,500,000 ?)
LAOS (1954)	236,800	3,611,000	Vientiane (90,000)
MALAYSIA (1963)	329,749	14,777,000	Kuala Lumpur (770,000)
PHILIPPINES (1946)	300,000	50,697,000	Manila (1,626,000)
SINGAPORE (1965)	581	2,476,000	Singapore (1,400,000)
THAILAND (—)	514,000	49,414,000	Bangkok (4,871,000)
VIETNAM (1954*)	329,556	51,742,000	Hanoi (2,000,000)

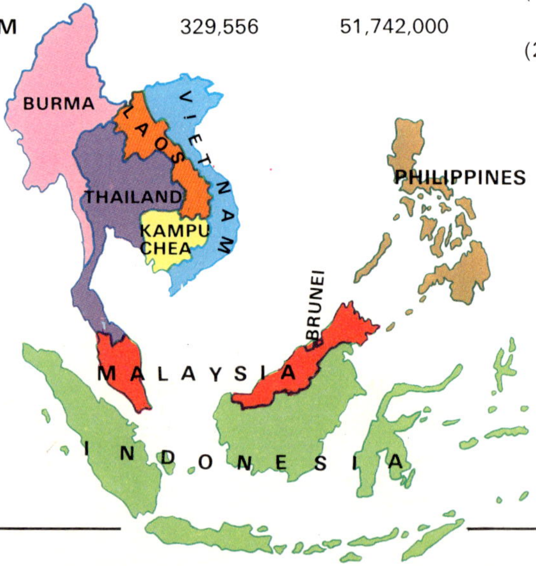

Highest point	Official language	Currency	Main exports
—	Malay	Brunei dollar	Oil
Hkakado Razi, 5881 m	Burmese	Kyat	Teak, oil cake, jute, rubber
Putjak Djaja, 4883 m	Bahasa (Indonesian)	Rupiah	Oil, coffee, rubber, palm products
Mt Ka-kup, 1744 m	Khmer	Riel	Rice, rubber
Phu Bia, 2820 m	Lao	Kip	Timber, coffee
Mt Kinabalu, 4102 m	Malay	Malaysian dollar	Rubber, tin, timber, palm oil
Mt Apo, 2954 m	Philipino	Peso	Coconut products, sugar, timber
Bukit Timah, 177 m	Malay, Chinese, Tamil, English	Singapore dollar	Refined petroleum products, electronic goods, rubber
Inthanon Peak, 2595 m	Thai	Baht	Rice, rubber, tapioca, tin
Fan Si Pan, 3143 m	Vietnamese	Dong	Coal, agricultural goods, fish

*Independent from France in 1954, partitioned into North and South Vietnam. Became a united Communist republic in 1976 after a long war.

Brunei

Burma

Indonesia

Kampuchea

Laos

Malaysia

Philippines

Singapore

Thailand

Vietnam

COLONIAL HISTORY AND RELIGION

Thailand: "Thailand ... has long maintained its sovereignty because the Thais have always been united ..." (Thai National Anthem). Thailand, once called Siam, is a kingdom which has remained independent when all the other countries were parts of European empires. Mostly Buddhist.

Vietnam, Laos and Kampuchea: Once these three countries made up French Indo-China. French withdrew in 1954. Vietnam was divided into two parts and a long civil war started between the North backed by the USSR and the South backed by the USA. The South fell to the North in 1975 and Vietnam became united as a Communist republic. Laos and Kampuchea (formerly Cambodia) are also now Communist Republics. All three countries are mainly Buddhist.

Malaysia and Singapore: Formerly British colonies. Malaysia was established in 1963 when Malaya, Singapore, Sabah and Sarawak formed a federation. Singapore became a separate republic in 1965. Malaysia is mainly Muslim but Singapore has many Buddhists, Taoists and Confucians.

Brunei: Independent monarchy 1983. Former British colony. Mostly Muslim.

Burma: Socialist Republic. Former British colony, independent 1948. Mostly Buddhist.

Indonesia: Once the Dutch East Indies. Independent 1949, adding Portuguese Timor in 1976. Mostly Muslim.

The Philippines: Under Spanish rule to 1898 then ceded to the USA. Independent 1946, the only mainly Christian country in Asia.

▼ **Rice** is intensively farmed on the terraced hillsides of Java in Indonesia.

INDONESIA

Indonesia, with twice as many people as any other country in S.E. Asia, has the fifth largest population in the world.

The country consists of over 13,000 islands, of which about 3000 are inhabited. The islands stretch over 5000 km from west of the Malay *peninsula* to the border of Papua-New Guinea. A mountain ridge runs through the islands, and Indonesia has more active *volcanoes* than any other country: 77 have erupted in recent times. Krakatoa, the volcano that exploded in 1883, was one of these islands. The volcanic soil is very rich.

Two-thirds of Indonesians live on Java, though the government is encouraging people to move to the less densely populated islands, especially Sumatra. There are many different groups of people in Indonesia, and over 70 languages are spoken. People on the island of Bali are Hindus. Their carvings and customs fascinate tourists.

RICE

Rice is the most important food crop in the world, and is especially important in the crowded islands of South-East Asia. There is evidence that it was grown in Thailand in 6000 BC.

Rice grows well in hot, wet countries. If the rainy season is long enough, farmers can grow two crops a year. Seedlings are grown in a 'nursery' bed, then transplanted by hand into flooded paddy-fields. This is hot, hard, tiring work and the water level must be carefully controlled. The terraced hillsides of South-East Asia are made by hand; the level is exactly right, and some are hundreds of years old. After four or five months the rice is ready to be harvested and the water is released. In most areas, rice is harvested by hand. The International Rice Research Institute in the Philippines has been developing new types of rice plants with short stems and more seeds. These IR types have dramatically improved rice yields throughout Asia, but they require lots of fertiliser and careful water control.

South Asia

The great mountain ranges of the Himalayas and the Hindu Kush separate South Asia from the rest of the continent. Nearly a billion people live in these eight countries, the largest of which is India.

From the mountains flow three great rivers. The Indus provides water for the *desert* country of Pakistan. The Ganges, a holy river to Hindus, flows through a densely populated *plain* in northern India. The Brahmaputra joins the Ganges to form a great *delta*, criss-crossed with water channels, in the country of Bangladesh. Most of southern India consists of the Deccan *plateau*, which ends at the steep Western Ghats overlooking the Arabian Sea, and the gentler Eastern Ghats overlooking the Bay of Bengal. A chain of sandy islands link India to the *tropical* island of Sri Lanka.

In all these countries, the majority of the people live in villages and rely on farming. Farmers prepare land for the expected arrival of the *monsoon*. But if the rain comes too soon, the crops may be washed away and the land flooded. If it comes late, there will be drought and the crops will not grow. The most crowded areas are the coasts of India and the Ganges Valley, where rainfall is reliable enough for good harvests: Bangladesh is one of the most densely populated countries in the world. Along with the land-locked mountain states, it is also one of the poorest.

As medicines to prevent many diseases have become available, the population of South Asia has risen dramatically. Great advances are being made in both agriculture and industry, but the problems of finding enough food and work remain.

C H I N A
K2
8611m
Karakoram Range
Amritsar
Lahore
TIBET
HIMALAYAS
Nanda Devi
7817m
Mt Everest, 8848m, is the highest mountain in the world
Mt Everest
8848m
SIKKIM
BHUTAN
NEPAL
Katmandu
Darjeeling
Mt Kanchenjunga
8598m
Brahmaputra
Delhi
Jaipur
Agra
Lucknow
Kanpur
Ganges
Allahabad
Varanasi
(Benares)
Patna
BANGLADESH
Dacca
Chittagong
Howrah
Calcutta
BURMA
Indore
Narmada
Nagpur
Mahanadi
INDIA
Poona
Godavari
Sholapur
Hyderabad
Krishna
Deccan
Eastern Ghats
Western Ghats
BAY OF BENGAL
Madras
Bangalore
Cochin
Madurai
Trivandrum
SRI LANKA
Colombo
2524
Kilometres
0
200
400
600
0
100
200
300
Miles
N

Country (Independent)	Area (in sq km)	Population	Capital (population)
AFGHANISTAN (—)	647,497	16,024,000	Kabul (749,000)
BANGLADESH (1971)	143,998	94,472,000	Dacca (2,000,000)
BHUTAN (—)	47,000	1,352,000	Thimphu (1,352,000)
INDIA (1947)	3,287,590	698,632,000	Delhi (3,647,000)
MALDIVES (1965) An island republic in the Indian Ocean about 650 km south-west of India.	298	167,000	Malé (30,000)
NEPAL (—)	140,797	14,932,000	Katmandu (195,000)
PAKISTAN (1947)	803,943	85,558,000	Islamabad (235,000)
SRI LANKA (1948)	65,610	15,398,000	Colombo (624,000)

RELIGION

India: Most people are Hindus but there are groups of Muslims, Christians, Sikhs and Jains.
Pakistan and Bangladesh: Mainly Muslim. When India became independent in 1947, the Muslim areas became East and West Pakistan with Hindu India in between. In 1971, East Pakistan became the separate country Bangladesh. Hindus, Buddhists and Christians live in each country.
Afghanistan: Mainly Muslim.
Bhutan: Buddhist and Hindu.
Maldives: Mainly Muslim.
Nepal: Mainly Hindu.
Sri Lanka: Mainly Buddhist with groups of Hindus, Christians and Muslims.

Afghanistan

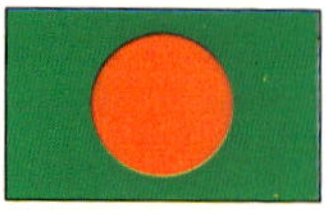
Bangladesh

Bhutan

India

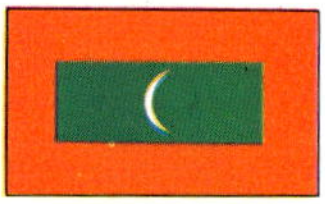
Maldives

Nepal

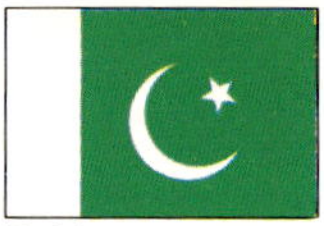
Pakistan

Sri Lanka

▶ **India:** a market in Benares.

Highest point	Official language	Currency	Main exports
Noshag, 7492 m	Pashtu and Dari	Afghani	Cotton, natural gas, fruit, skins
Keokradong, 1230 m	Bengali	Taka	Jute, hides and skins, leather, tea
Khula Kangri, 7554 m	Dzongkha	Ngultrum	Rice, fruit, timber
Nanda Devi, 7817 m	Hindi, English	Rupee	Textiles, jute, tea, industrial goods
—	Divehi	Rupee	Copra (from coconuts), fish
Everest, 8848 m	Nepali	Rupee	Grains, timber, cattle, hides
Godwin Austen, 8611 m	Urdu	Rupee	Cotton, textiles, rice, carpets and rugs, leather
Pidurutalagala, 2527 m	Sinhala	Rupee	Tea, rubber, coconut products, industrial goods

AGRICULTURE

Farming is the source of income of the great majority of people in all of South Asia. Farms are often small with the land divided into tiny plots. Many farmers are tenants of rich landowners and give part of their crops as rent.
Water: The water supply is often a problem. Most farmers depend on the *monsoon* rains. These are often unreliable, especially in the Deccan and in north-west India and Pakistan. *Irrigation* schemes have improved the farming in many areas. In the south large reservoirs (tanks) are common. In many areas wells are used or channels leading from rivers that have been dammed. Pakistan relies on water from the Indus for almost all its agriculture.
Food crops: Rice is important wherever there is enough water from rain or irrigation. It is especially important in Sri Lanka, Bangladesh, the coasts of India and the lower Ganges valley, and in the valleys of Nepal and Bhutan. Wheat is important in Pakistan and the drier north-west of India. Millet grows on poorer soil, as in the Deccan.
Cash crops: Cotton is grown in dry areas for textile industry, jute in the Ganges delta, tea in the hills of India and Sri Lanka, rubber and coffee in Sri Lanka and south India. Sugar cane, groundnuts and other oil-seeds and spices also grown. Grapes for dried fruit in Afghanistan.
Animals: India has lots of cattle, but they are not used for meat as they are sacred to Hindus. They provide leather. Oxen, mules and camels are draught animals. Sheep raising is important in dry areas – especially in Afghanistan.

▼ **Bangladesh:** planting rice seedlings in a paddy field.

▶ **Sri Lanka:** picking the tender leaves of the tea plant.

INDUSTRY

India:
The most industrialized country in the area and the world's 10th largest industrial nation. Products range from cotton cloth to space satellites.
Minerals: Plenty of coal and iron ore, manganese and other metals; mica; some oil.
Industrial areas: Heavy industry important west of Calcutta. Textiles near Bombay. Light industries in south.
Other Countries:
These have developing industries, mainly based on *cash crops* (rubber in Sri Lanka; cotton textiles in Pakistan) and local needs (bricks, cement, food and drink, tobacco). Pakistan has natural gas and *hydro-electricity.* There is very little industry in the landlocked mountain states – Afghanistan, Bhutan and Nepal. Afghanistan, has less than 1% of working population in factories, and earns more from handicraft goods.

MONSOON CLIMATE

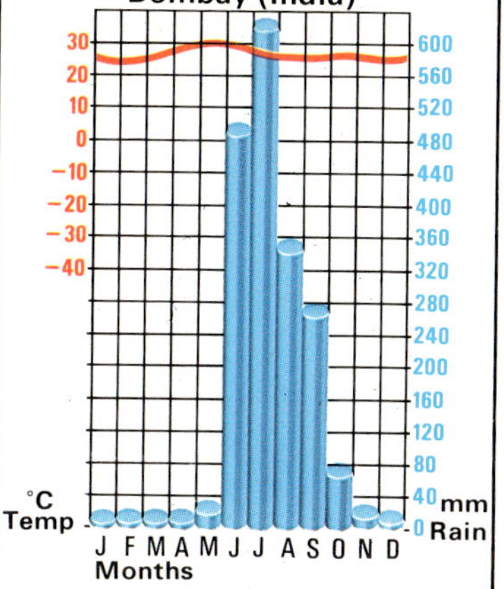

The three seasons are cool and dry (October to March); hot and dry (April to mid-June); and hot and wet (June to September). This rainy season occurs in most of South Asia and is called the monsoon. It begins suddenly, with winds blowing from the warm sea to the dry land. The air turns cooler and there is rain for crops.

Istanbul
BLACK SEA
USSR
CASPIAN SEA
Ankara
Mt Ararat
5165
TURKEY
Izmir
Tabriz
Adana
Elburz
Halab
(Aleppo)
Mosul
CYPRUS
Nicosia
Tigris
SYRIA
LEBANON
Mesopotamia
MEDITERRANEAN
SEA
Beirut
Damascus
Baghdad
Zagros Mts
ISRAEL
Tel Aviv
IRAQ
Jerusalem
Amman
Euphrates
Suez
Canal
JORDAN
Abadan
Basra
EGYPT
KUWAIT
Dead Sea
392m below
sea level
PERSIAN
BAHRAIN
RED SEA
Kilometres
0 100 200 300 400
N
0 100 200
Miles
Medina
Riyadh
SAUDI
ARABIA
Jidda
Mecca
SUDAN
Rub'al Khali (Empty
YEMEN
A.R.
YEMEN
P.D.R.
San'a
Aden
ETHIOPIA
GULF OF ADEN
DJIBOUTI

South-West Asia

The south-western part of Asia is usually called the Middle East. Here, Asia joins on to Africa and Europe. Most of the land is *desert*, and thinly populated. Vast areas, such as Rub'al Khali, 'the Empty Quarter', are uninhabited. Much of Turkey and Iran is high *plateau* land, and in the mountains temperatures can be very low. High land borders the Red Sea, too. The main rivers, the Tigris and the Euphrates, form a fertile lowland in Iraq. Ruins of ancient civilizations have been found here.

Where *irrigation* is possible, fine crops of dates, fruit, cotton, lentils and cereals such as barley and wheat are grown. Some ancient water channels and storage systems are still in use, but modern irrigation schemes are being developed in all these countries.

Oil resources make some of these sparsely populated countries among the richest in the world. Wealth from the sale of oil is being used for many development projects such as new airports, roads, factories, schools and hospitals. To improve the water supply, desalination plants have been built in some countries to turn sea water into fresh water. People from Europe and from other Islamic countries of Asia have come to work on new projects.

Country	Area (in sq km)	Population	Capital (population)
BAHRAIN	622	467,000	Manama (114,000)
CYPRUS	9,251	665,000	Nicosia (121,000)
IRAN	1,648,000	40,288,000	Tehran (4,496,000)
IRAQ	434,924	13,977,000	Baghdad (3,206,000)
ISRAEL	20,770	4,093,000	Jerusalem (398,000)
JORDAN	97,740	3,403,000	Amman (750,000)
KUWAIT	17,818	1,516,000	Kuwait (400,000)
LEBANON	10,400	3,325,000	Beirut (702,000)
OMAN	212,457	950,000	Muscat (7000)
QATAR	11,000	294,000	Doha (130,000)
SAUDI ARABIA	2,149,690	9,418,000	Riyadh (669,000)
SYRIA	185,180	9,227,000	Damascus (1,042,000)
TURKEY	780,576	47,663,000	Ankara (1,236,000)
UNITED ARAB EMIRATES	83,600	1,040,000	Abu Dhabi (250,000)
YEMEN ARAB REPUBLIC	195,000	6,142,000	San'a (448,000)
YEMEN PDR	332,968	1,905,000	Aden (264,000)

Bahrain

Cyprus

Iran

Iraq

Israel

Jordan

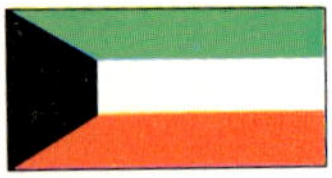
Kuwait

Lebanon

Official language	Currency	Government	Main exports
Arabic	Dinar	Sheikdom	Petroleum (oil)
Greek and Turkish	Pound	Republic	Fruit, vegetables, wine, manufactured goods, minerals
Persian (Farsi)	Rial	Islamic Republic	Oil, natural gas, cotton
Arabic	Iraqi dinar	Republic	Oil, dates, wool, cotton
Hebrew, Arabic	Shekel	Republic	Cut diamonds, chemicals, fruit, fruit juice, tobacco
Arabic	Jordanian dinar	Kingdom	Phosphates, fruit, vegetables
Arabic	Kuwait dinar	Emirate	Oil
Arabic	Lebanese pound	Republic	Jewellery, precious metals and gemstones, textiles
Arabic	Omani, riyal	Sultanate	Oil, dates, tobacco, frankincense
Arabic	Qatar riyal	Emirate	Oil
Arabic	Riyal	Kingdom	Oil
Arabic	Syrian pound	Republic	Cotton, oil, cereals, animals
Turkish	Turkish lira	Republic	Cotton, nuts, fruit, tobacco
Arabic	Dirham	Independent Federation	Oil, gas
Arabic	Riyal	Republic	Cotton, coffee, hides and skins
Arabic	Dinar	Marxist Republic	Cotton, fish, refined oil

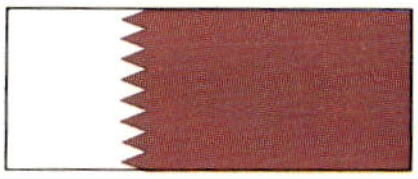
Qatar

Oman

Saudi Arabia

Syria

Turkey

UAE

Yemen AR

Yemen PDR

INDUSTRY AND FARMING

Minerals:
Oil (petroleum) accounts for the wealth of many countries in the Middle East. It is a fossil fuel formed millions of years ago by chemical action on the remains of plants and animals. Oil collects in *porous* layers of *sedimentary rocks* and can be obtained by drilling wells and pumping out the oil. The oil is then refined into petroleum for vehicles and fuel oil and to make a great variety of chemicals, including plastics. But both oil production and refining employ fairly few people. Natural gas is often found in the same place as oil.

Oil is a non-renewable resource. Once it is pumped out it cannot be replaced. Some of the wealth from oil is being used to establish new industries and farming for the day will come when the Middle East has no oil.
OPEC: This stands for the Organisation of Petroleum Exporting Countries. Founded by Iraq in 1960, its headquarters are in Austria. Founder members are Iraq, Iran, Kuwait, Saudi Arabia and Venezuela. Membership now also includes Algeria, Ecuador, Gabon, Indonesia, Libya, Nigeria, Qatar, United Arab Emirates. Members meet to discuss matters of concern to oil exporters, including prices, production and politics. They also give cash aid to less developed countries.

Farming:
Water supply is a problem in most areas. Crops are grown mainly in coastal areas where there is rain and places where wells, springs or rivers provide water for *irrigation*. Israel has orchards watered by complex irrigation schemes. In drier areas sheep and goats are kept for meat and dairy products.
Main crops: Fruit such as oranges, apples and grapes (Israel, Lebanon, Turkey), wheat, barley, tobacco, cotton (Turkey), dates (Iraq), lentils (Turkey, Iraq).

DESERT CLIMATE

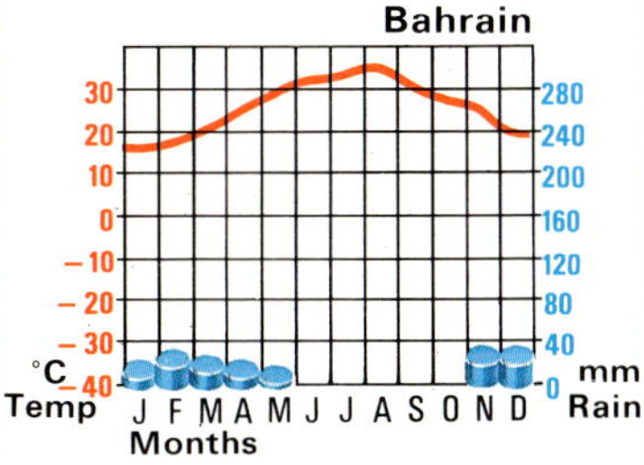

Bahrain is a true *desert* island. This graph shows that in several months NO rain is expected – and in other months the total will come in just one or two storms. The average total for the whole year is only 81 millimetres – some years will have even less rain than that. Bahrain is not an empty desert because, with money earned from oil, factories have been built to make fresh water from the sea. But large areas of the Middle East have even less rain and are almost deserted desert.

RELIGION

The Middle East is the home of three great religions: Judaism, Christianity and Islam. Followers of all three religions believe in one God and in peace but there have been many wars between them.

Judaism: This is the religion of the Jews. Most people in Israel are Jewish. Many of them are descendents of European Jews who settled there after World War II. The present Israeli nation was established in 1948. Before that the area was called Palestine and ruled by Britain.

Christianity: In Lebanon and Cyprus about half the people are Christians. There are many Christian holy places such as Bethlehem and Nazareth.

Islam: Almost everyone else in this region follows the Islamic religion. Muslims worship one God whom they call Allah, and believe Muhammed was God's special prophet. Islam's holy book is the Koran (Qur'an) written by Muhammed in Arabic. As Islam spread from the Middle East to many other countries, Arabic became the language of many people.

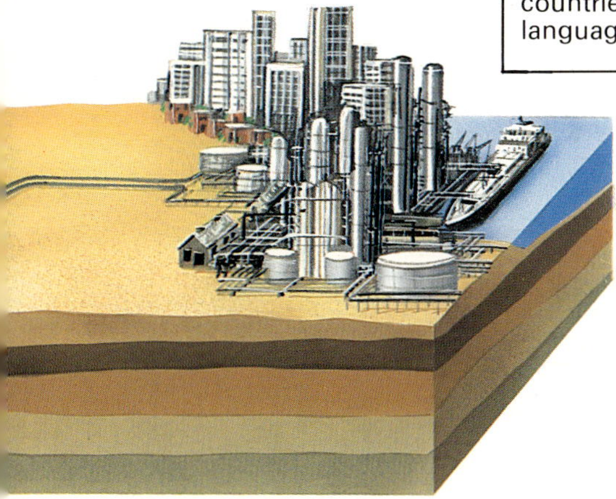

◀ **Oil is pumped** from deep beneath the desert where the rock layers have been bent upwards into an anticline. The surplus gas is burnt off and then the oil is pumped through pipelines to the coast. Here, it is refined or exported as crude oil in giant oil tankers.

Africa

Africa is a huge continent – more than 7000 kilometres long and 6000 kilometres wide. Except in the high mountains it is hot everywhere, but there are great differences in rainfall and in type of vegetation.

Most of Africa is a *plateau*. There are two *deserts* – the Sahara in the north and the much smaller Namib in the south. Much of the rest of the land is *savanna* grassland with tall grass and thorny bushes. Near the Equator, the lowlands are covered with *tropical* forest.

Centuries ago, great empires flourished in Africa. Some of the names are used as names of new countries, such as Mali, Benin, Ghana and Zimbabwe. Then in the 1880s European countries explored and colonized Africa. It took until the 1960s for most of Africa to regain its independence, and the 80 years of European control have had a lasting effect. The boundaries of most African countries are still the ones fixed in Europe 100 years ago.

Today there are big cities throughout Africa, with modern offices and factories. But most people rely on farming. Away from the cities, African farmers are often struggling to grow enough to eat.

AREA:
30,319,000 sq km.
POPULATION:
484,000,000
INDEPENDENT COUNTRIES: 53
HIGHEST POINT:
Mt Kilimanjaro (5895 m).
LOWEST POINT:
Lake Assal in Djibouti (155 m below sea level).
LARGEST LAKE:
Lake Victoria (69,484 sq km).
LONGEST RIVERS:
Nile (6670 km), Zaire (4700 km), Niger (4184 km).
RICHEST COUNTRY
(GNP per person – see p. 19):
Libya ($8210).
POOREST COUNTRIES:
Chad ($120), Ethiopia ($130).

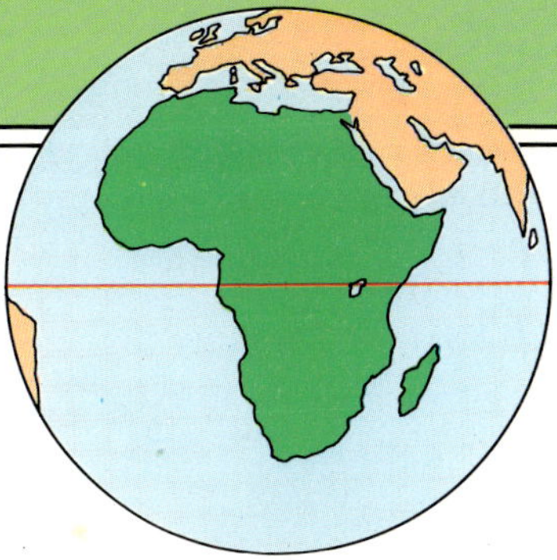

▶ **These women** are working hard to prepare the day's food in a village in Ghana. This is a common sight in tropical Africa.

◀ **The ruins of Zimbabwe** The name of this great empire of the past has now been given to a modern African country.

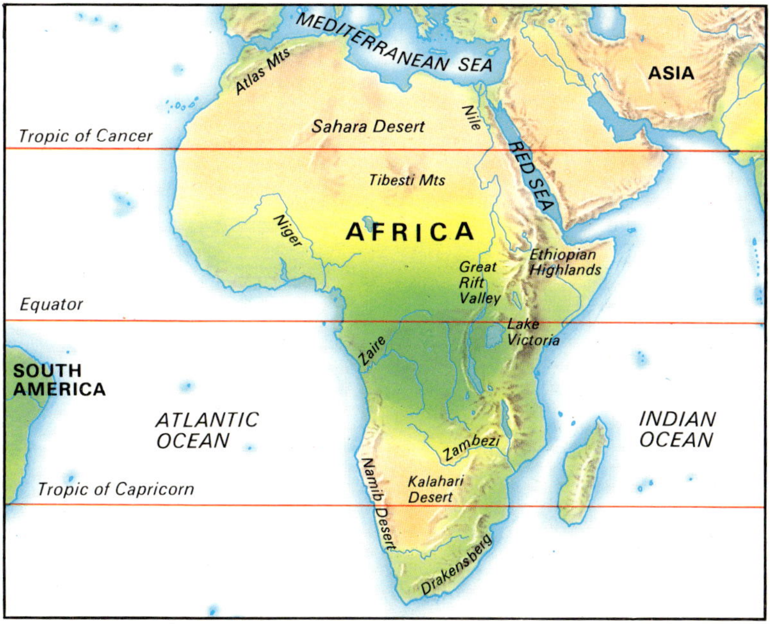

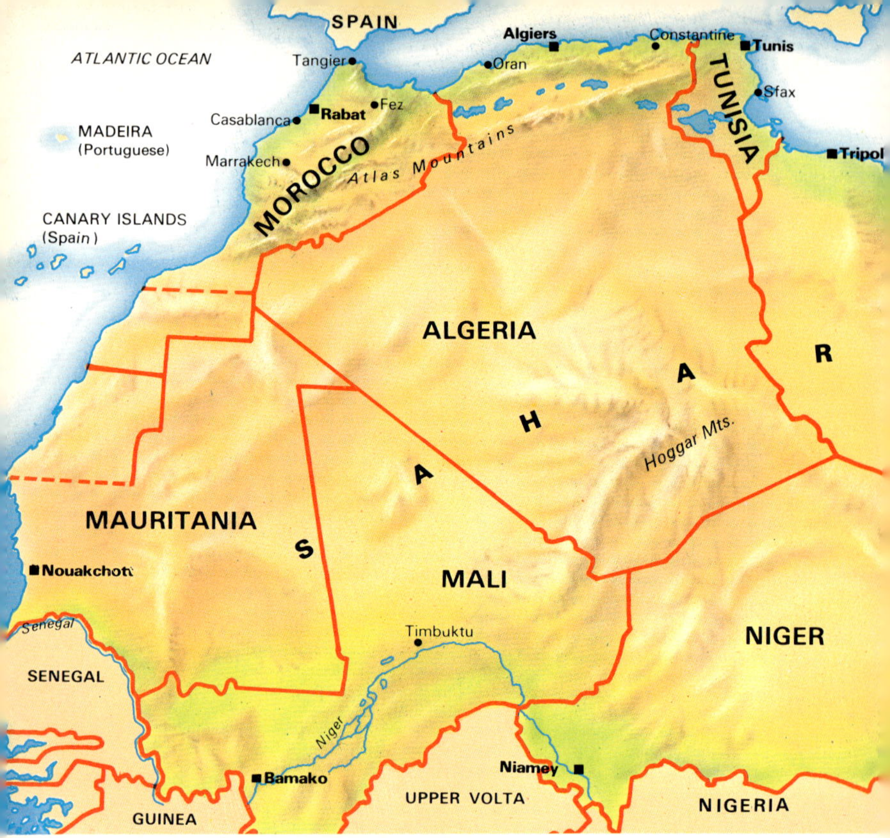

Northern Africa

Northern Africa is mainly a huge desert – the Sahara. Vast areas are empty, with only occasional *oasis* settlements. Nevertheless, over 160 million people live in the area shown on this map.

Five countries have over 20 million people. In Morocco and Algeria most people live north of the Sahara, where there is enough winter rain for crops to grow. In Ethiopia, people live in the mountains which have a rainy season. In Egypt and northern Sudan everyone lives in the *desert* but water from the river Nile is available for *irrigating* crops.

A few modern settlements exist deep in the desert where valuable minerals are found. These mineral resources are the main reason why some countries are richer than others. Oil-rich Libya is one of the wealthiest countries in the world. But Niger, Chad, Mali and Ethiopia are among the world's poorest countries.

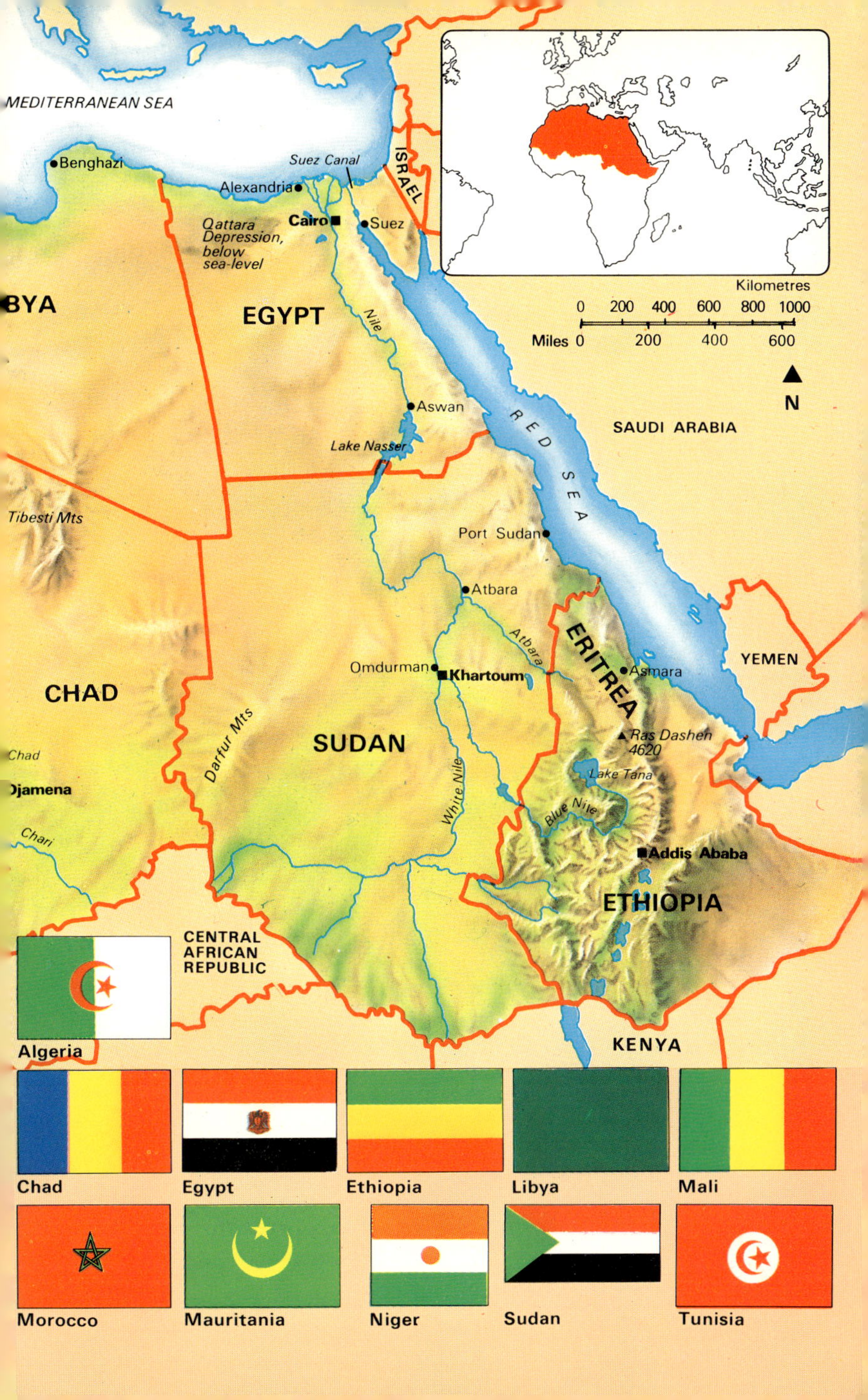
MEDITERRANEAN SEA
Benghazi
Suez Canal
Alexandria
ISRAEL
Cairo
Suez
Qattara Depression, below sea-level
BYA
EGYPT
Nile
Kilometres
0 200 400 600 800 1000
Miles 0 200 400 600
N
Aswan
SAUDI ARABIA
RED SEA
Lake Nasser
Tibesti Mts
Port Sudan
Atbara
Atbara
ERITREA
YEMEN
Omdurman
Khartoum
Asmara
CHAD
Darfur Mts
SUDAN
Ras Dashen 4620
Chad
Djamena
White Nile
Lake Tana
Blue Nile
Chari
Addis Ababa
ETHIOPIA
CENTRAL AFRICAN REPUBLIC
KENYA
Algeria
Chad
Egypt
Ethiopia
Libya
Mali
Morocco
Mauritania
Niger
Sudan
Tunisia

Country (Independent)	Area (in sq km)	Population	Capital (population)
ALGERIA (1962)	2,381,741	20,042,000	Algiers (1,503,700)
CHAD (1960)	1,284,000	4,714,000	N'Djamena (242,000)
EGYPT (1922)	1,001,449	43,611,000	Cairo (5,715,000)
ETHIOPIA (—)	1,221,900	34,244,000	Addis Ababa (1,104,000)
LIBYA (1951)	1,759,540	3,244,000	Tripoli (837,000)
MALI (1960)	1,240,000	6,966,000	Bamako (404,000)
MAURITANIA (1960)	1,030,700	1,721,000	Nouakchott (135,000)
MOROCCO (1956)	446,550 Excluding Western Sahara (area: 266,000 sq km; population: 165,000).	21,280,000	Rabat (368,000)
NIGER (1960)	1,267,000	5,600,000	Niamey (225,000)
SUDAN (1956)	2,505,813	19,373,000	Khartoum (1,000,000)
TUNISIA (1956)	163,610	6,625,000	Tunis (550,000)

GOVERNMENT

Before independence, France controlled most of these countries, and French is still spoken. The exceptions were: Libya (Italian), Morocco (partly Spanish), Egypt (British), Sudan (Anglo-Egyptian). Ethiopia has always been independent. Now all these countries are independent republics, except for Morocco which is a monarchy. Long before the French arrived, much of this area was conquered by the Arabs. Arabic is an important language and Islam the religion of most people.

RECORD FACTS

The Desert:
Record shade temperature: Libya 58°C in 1922.
Hottest place all year: Dallol, Ethiopia, averages 34·4° all year.
Sunniest place: Eastern Sahara, 4300 hours a year.
Highest sand dune: 430 m high in central Algeria.
Oldest university: Fez, Morocco, founded 859 AD

▶ **Tunisia:** selling oranges in the market at Sousse. Fruit grows well near the North African coast.

Highest point	Official language	Currency	Main exports
Mt Tahat, 2918 m	Arabic	Algerian dinar	Petroleum, natural gas
Emi Koussi, 3415 m	French	Franc CFA	Cotton, meat cattle
Jabul Katrinah, 2637 m	Arabic	Egyptian pound	Cotton, textiles, petroleum
Ras Dashan, 4620 m	Amharic	Ethiopian dollar	Coffee, hides and skins
Mt Bette, 2286 m	Arabic	Libyan dinar	Petroleum
Hombori Tondo, 1155 m	French	Mali franc	Cotton, ground-nuts
Kediet Ijill, 915 m	Arabic and French	Ouguiya	Iron ore
Mt Toubkal, 4165 m	Arabic	Dirham	Phosphates, fruit
Mt Greboun, 2000 m	French	Franc CFA	Uranium, animals
Mt Kinyeti, 3187 m	Arabic	Sudanese Pound	Cotton, ground-nuts
Djebel Chambi, 1544 m	Arabic	Tunisian dinar	Petroleum, olive oil, phosphates

PRODUCTS

Minerals: Oil: Important in Libya and Algeria; small amounts in Tunisia and Egypt. Phosphates: In Tunisia and Morocco. Iron ore and copper: Mined in Mauritania. Uranium: Found in Niger.
Agriculture: Only possible where there is water: with rainfall on the Mediterranean coast and in the Ethiopian highlands; with *irrigation* in oases, the Nile and other river valleys. Animal herding is the only productive use of the semi-desert. Farming occupies very little land, but a lot of people.
Main crops: Citrus fruits and olives (Mediterranean coast); dates (*oases*); cotton (Egypt, Sudan, Chad, Mali); rice (Egypt); coffee (Ethiopia); groundnuts (Sudan). Many local food crops grown.
Industry: Very little modern industry except in the countries bordering the Mediterranean Sea.
Tourism: Important in Morocco, Tunisia and Egypt. The sunshine and the many ancient monuments in all these countries attract visitors.

► **Chad:** herdsmen bring their cattle to a well in the semi-desert.

▼ **Egypt:** the River Nile is the source of water for crops and for drinking. Away from the river where the water cannot reach to irrigate, the land is desert.

NATURAL FEATURES

The Sahara Desert: Covers about 8,400,000 sq km, the world's largest *desert.* About a tenth is sand *dunes*; the rest gravel or rock desert. Dry valleys *(wadis)* cross many parts. Cave-paintings of animals suggest that the desert was once much wetter. Now it is increasing in area: people plant trees and spray oil on dunes to stop them advancing, but overgrazing by goats and cattle means the desert continues to grow. Where there is water there are *oases*: date palms and many other crops are grown there.

Mountains: Atlas Mts in north-west reach over 4000 m. Hoggar and Tibesti Mts in central Sahara reach over 3000 m. Ethiopian Highlands are high *plateau* with large areas over 3000 m and mountains reaching over 4000 m.

Lakes: Hardly exist in such a dry area. Lake Chad looks like a huge inland sea on the map: it is very shallow (average depth 4 m) and marshy. Important locally for its fish.

River Nile: The world's longest river – 6670 km. If flows all year and almost all Egyptians are crowded into its valley and *delta.* Since ancient times, Egyptians have relied on its water for *irrigation.* The White Nile flows from Lake Victoria (Uganda) where it rains most of the year. The Blue Nile rises in Ethiopia; the heavy rains in July and August make the river flood. This annual flood was very important in Egypt. Now it is controlled by several dams; the largest is the Aswan Dam which holds back Lake Nasser.

Suez Canal: 162 km long, it joins the Mediterranean and the Red Sea to make a short sea-route from Europe to Asia. Built by a Frenchman, Ferdinand de Lesseps, it was opened in 1869. The canal has no locks. Its course includes the Bitter Lakes.

West Africa

Benin

Cameroon

Congo

Gabon

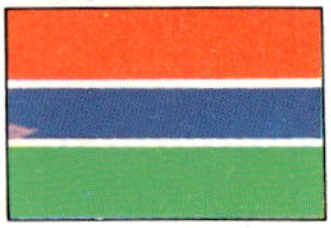

Gambia

Ghana

The coastlands of West Africa are hot with a long wet season. *Rain forest* covers much of the area. The climate and diseases such as malaria and yellow fever made it difficult for Europeans to settle here, but they did build some ports and forts. Names like Gold Coast (now Ghana), Ivory Coast and Slave Coast give clues to the trade on which they lived.

Many people in this coastal area are farmers. Tree-crops are important money-earners, especially cocoa, coffee, palm oil and rubber. Root crops such as cassava and yams are grown for food.

Inland, the forest gives way to *savanna* grassland, with trees like the baobab which can survive the long, hot dry season. The main food crops here are cereals, such as millet, maize and sorghum. Groundnuts and cotton are important cash crops, and cattle are kept for their hides and skins as well as for meat.

All these West African countries export raw materials – either crops or minerals. They do not have much industry, and have to import manufactured goods. But the income they receive for their raw materials does not match the cost of imported manufactured goods, so it is often difficult to earn enough money for development. To overcome this problem, each country is trying to establish industries. The ports are the main centres of development.

Guinea

Ivory Coast

Liberia

Nigeria

▼ **Ghana:** Women winnow the rice left behind after the field has been harvested.

Senegal

Sierra Leone

Togo

Upper Volta

Country (Independent)	Area (in sq km)	Population	Capital (population)	Official language
BENIN (1960)	112,622	3,734,000	Porto Novo (104,000)	French
CAMEROON (1960)	475,442	8,804,000	Yaounde (314,000)	French and English
CAPE VERDE ISLANDS (1975)	4033	324,000	Praia (21,000)	Portuguese
CONGO (1960)	342,000	1,613,000	Brazzaville (301,000)	French
EQUATORIAL GUINEA (1968)	28,051	378,000	Malabo (37,000)	Spanish
GABON (1980)	267,667	667,000	Libreville (251,000)	French
GAMBIA (1965)	11,295	642,000	Banjul (39,000)	English
GHANA (1957)	238,537	12,413,000	Accra (738,000)	English
GUINEA (1958)	245,957	5,741,000	Conakry (526,000)	French
GUINEA-BISSAU (1974)	36,125	817,000	Bissau (109,000)	Portuguese
IVORY COAST (1960)	322,463	9,564,000	Abidjan (686,000)	French
LIBERIA (1847)	111,369	1,992,000	Monrovia (220,000)	English
NIGERIA (1960)	923,768	88,847,000	*Lagos (Abuja) (1,061,000)	English
SAO TOME & PRINCIPE (1975)	965	110,000	Sao Tome (17,000)	Portuguese
SENEGAL (1960)	196,192	5,967,000	Dakar (800,000)	French
SIERRE LEONE (1961)	71,740	3,643,000	Freetown (274,000)	English
TOGO (1960)	56,000	2,693,000	Lome (229,000)	French
UPPER VOLTA (1960)	274,200	5,917,000	Ouagadougou (173,000)	French

Currency	Main exports
Franc CFA	Cotton, cocoa
Franc CFA	Coffee, cocoa, petroleum
Escudo	Fish, bananas
Franc CFA	Petroleum, timber
Ekuele	Cocoa, coffee
Franc CFA	Petroleum, manganese
Dalasi	Groundnuts
Cedi	Cocoa, timber, gold
Syli	Bauxite, alumina
Escudo	Groundnuts, fish
Franc CFA	Coffee, cocoa, timber
Liberian dollar	Iron ore, rubber
Naira	Petroleum, palm kernels, cocoa
Dobra	Cocoa
Franc CFA	Groundnuts, phosphates
Leone	Diamonds, iron ore
Franc CFA	Phosphates, cocoa, coffee
Franc CFA	Cotton, animals, groundnuts

FOOD CROPS

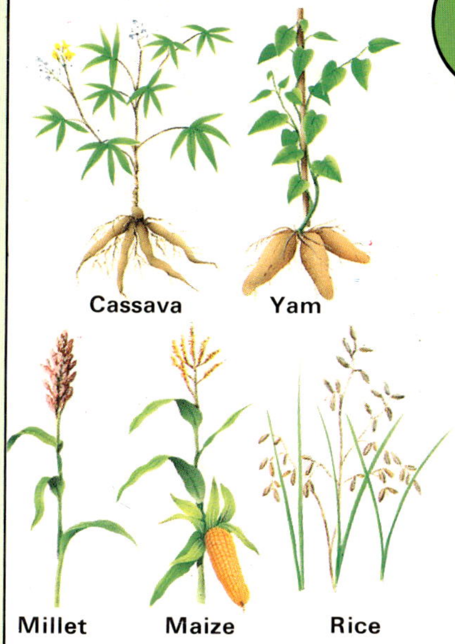

CASH CROPS

*Nigeria is scheduled to have a new capital in the 1980s.

Central and East Africa

There are several quite different types of scenery in Central Africa and East Africa. Much of Central Africa is lowland. The river Zaire (once called the Congo) is one of Africa's mighty rivers. With its tributaries, it drains a huge area of Central Africa and is important for transport except where there are rapids. The lowland areas are covered with dense *rain forest*. Here, people live in small clearings where they grow cassava, yams and other food crops. In some places the forest is being cleared for timber such as mahogany and okoumé, but the heavy rains soon wash the soil away if it is not protected. Most *cash crops* are from trees: rubber, cocoa, palm oil and coffee. But Zaire's main wealth comes from the copper mines in the south-east of the country.

In contrast, East Africa is mainly high land with *savanna* grassland. The top of the East African *plateau* is pleasantly cool and in the past Europeans settled here to grow *cash crops* like tea, cotton, coffee and sisal on large farms. Maize, millet and plantains (green bananas used as a vegetable) are the main food crops. The savanna lands of East Africa are famous for wild animals. Lions, elephants, zebra and rhinos were hunted in the past, but are now protected in large game reserves.

Somalia and Djibouti are *desert* lands forming the Horn of Africa. In both countries, most people are animal herders and many are very poor. Because of the fighting in this part of Africa, many people are also homeless refugees.

▶ **Giraffe** among the thorn bushes of the savanna near Mt Kilimanjaro.

SUDAN
N
RED SEA
DJIBOUTI
Djibouti
Shibeli
ETHIOPIA
SOMALI REPUBLIC
Lake Turkana
UGANDA
Range
Ruwenzori
5109m
Kisangani
Kampala
KENYA
Mogadishu
Juba
5199m
Kismaju
ZAIRE
Lake Victoria
Nairobi
Kigali
RWANDA
Mt Kilimanjaro
5894m
Bujumbura
BURUNDI
Mombasa
INDIAN OCEAN
PEMBA
TANZANIA
ZANZIBAR
Lualaba
Lake Tanganyika
Dodoma
Dar-es-Salaam
Kilometres
0 200 400 600 800
0 250 500
Miles
Songea
COMOROS
Lubumbashi
MALAWI
Lake Malawi
MOZAMBIQUE
ZAMBIA

Burundi

CAR

Djibouti

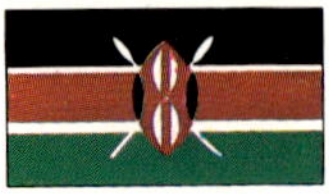

Kenya

Country (Independent)	Area (in sq km)	Population	Capital (population)
BURUNDI (1962)	27,834	4,293,000	Bujumbura (157,000)
CENTRAL AFRICAN REPUBLIC (1960)	622,984	2,086,000	Bangui (302,000)
DJIBOUTI (1977)	22,000	371,000	Djibouti (150,000)
KENYA (1963)	582,646	16, 922,000	Nairobi (700,000)
RWANDA (1962)	26,338	5,067,000	Kigali (118,000)
SEYCHELLES (1976) *A group of islands in the Indian Ocean.	280	70,000	Victoria (23,000)
SOMALI REPUBLIC (1960)	637,657	4,125,000	Mogadishu (400,000)
TANZANIA (1962)	945,087	19,388,000	Dodoma (25,000)
UGANDA (1962)	236,036	13,983,000	Kampala (350,000)
ZAIRE (1960)	2,345,409	29,826,000	Kinshasa (2,444,000)

SAVANNA CLIMATE

Songea is in southern Tanzania, 10° south of the Equator. The hottest time of year is from October to March, but the people here do not speak of summer and winter: it is hot all through the year. Instead they talk about the wet and dry seasons – and the graph shows you why: for six months there is very little rain.

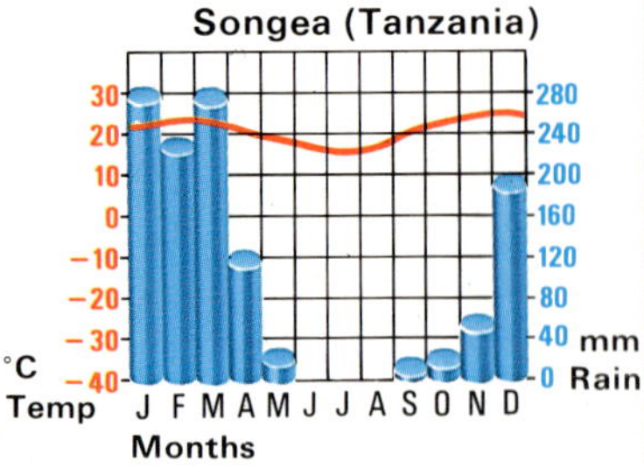

Rwanda

Tanzania

Uganda

Zaire

Highest point	Official language	Currency	Main exports
2865 m	French, Kirundi	Burundi franc	Coffee
Mt Gaou, 1420 m	French	Franc CFA	Coffee, timber, diamonds
	French	Djibouti franc	Hides and skins, cattle
Mt Kenya, 5199 m	English, Swahili	Kenya shilling	Coffee, tea, hides
4507 m	French, Kinyarwanda	Rwanda franc	Coffee
Mt Seychelles, 912 m	English, French	Rupee	Copra, spices, fish
Erigavo, 2406 m	Somali	Somali shilling	Animals
Mt Kilimanjaro, 5895 m	English, Swahili	Tanzanian shilling	Coffee, spices, sisal, cotton
Mt Stanley, 5109 m	English	Ugandan shilling	Coffee, cotton
5109 m	French	Zaire	Copper, cobalt, coffee

NATURAL FEATURES

Part of the Great Rift Valley is in East Africa. A *rift valley* forms when land sinks between faults in the earth's crust. The great rift valley is over 4800 km long: it begins in Syria, includes the Jordan Valley, Dead Sea, Red Sea, and then runs through Ethiopia, Kenya and Malawi. A second branch runs through Uganda and Tanzania. In the Rift Valley is a chain of long narrow lakes including Turkana, Mobutu, Tanganyika, and Malawi. East Africa's largest lake, Lake Victoria (69,500 sq km), was formed by subsidence. Earth movements also helped to form *volcanoes*: Mt Kilimanjaro (5895 m), Mt Kenya (5199 m) and others in the Ruwenzori Range.

Southern Africa

Most of Southern Africa is high and flat. *Savanna* grassland covers most of the *plateau*, and there are huge game reserves for wild animals. In the west, most of Namibia is *desert* and semi-desert, while on the east coast it is hot and wet and forest flourishes. In the south-east, the plateau ends with a high mountain range called the Drakensberg.

Southern Africa is very rich in minerals. Gold found near Johannesburg last century started a gold rush. Europeans came to get rich, and many stayed to develop mines and industries, and to own land for farming. Because of the number of white settlers and the richness of the land, it has been harder for black Africans to gain the independence of their countries. South Africa is still a country where political and economic power is held by a white minority.

In all parts, most people are farmers, growing crops for themselves and sometimes for export. In grassland areas, especially in Botswana and Lesotho, cattle rearing is important.

The great rivers of southern Africa are being dammed for *hydro-electric power*. The Zambezi has two huge dams – Kariba and Cabora Bassa. The Orange River in South Africa is being dammed to provide power and water for *irrigation*.

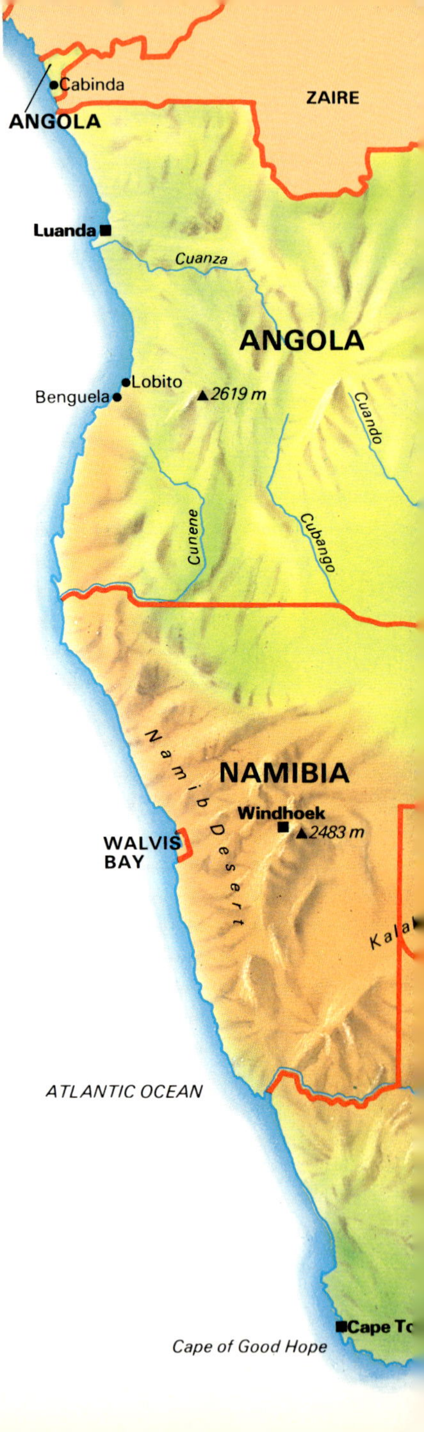

Kilometres
0
200
400
600
N
0
100
200
300
Miles
COMOROS
Lake Mweru
Lake Bangweulu
MALAWI
Lake Nyasa (Lake Malawi)
Kitwe
ZAMBIA
Lilongwe
MOZAMBIQUE
Mocambique
Cabora Bassa
Lusaka
Blantyre
Lake Kariba
Zambezi
Harare
Victoria Falls
ZIMBABWE
Bulawayo
Beira
INDIAN OCEAN
Diego Suarez
2876m
BOTSWANA
Limpopo
MOZAMBIQUE CHANNEL
Gaborone
Pretoria
Johannesburg
Mbabane
Maputo
MADAGASCAR
Antananarivo
SWAZILAND
Vaal
LESOTHO
Kimberley
3299m
Bloemfontein
Maseru
Durban
REPUBLIC OF SOUTH AFRICA
Drakensberg
East London
Port Elizabeth

Angola

Botswana

Lesotho

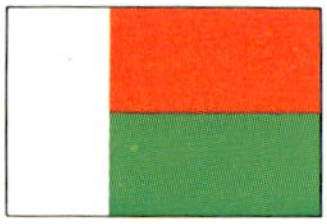
Madagascar

Malawi

Country (Independent)	Area (in sq km)	Population	Capital (population)
ANGOLA (1975)	1,246,700	7,414,000	Luanda (481,000)
BOTSWANA (1966)	600,372	820,000	Gaborone (54,000)
COMOROS (1975)	2,171	343,000	Moroni (12,000)
LESOTHO (1966)	30,355	1,406,000	Maseru (60,000)
MADAGASCAR (1960)	587,041	9,167,000	Antananarivo (400,000)
MALAWI (1964)	118,484	6,376,000	Lilongwe (103,000)
MOZAMBIQUE (1975)	783,030	10,987,000	Maputo (355,000)
NAMIBIA Ruled by South Africa but claimed by the UN as a trusteeship.	824,292	1.066,000	Windhoek (76,000)
SOUTH AFRICA (1934)	1,221,037	30,844,000	Cape Town (1,097,000) Pretoria (562,000)
SWAZILAND (1968)	17,363	581,000	Mbabane (22,000)
ZAMBIA (1964)	752,614	5,992,000	Lusaka (659,000)
ZIMBABWE (1979)	390,580	7,878,000	Harare (616,000)

MINING IN SOUTHERN AFRICA

The oldest known mines in the world are in Swaziland where iron was mined 43,000 years ago.

Diamonds: Found in volcanic rocks. The largest is the Cullinan diamond, found in Pretoria in 1905. South Africa still mines diamonds today; also Botswana Angola, Lesotho, Namibia.

Gold: South Africa's main export. The richest gold mines in the world are in Transvaal. The gold mines employ Africans who travel hundreds of miles from nearby countries.

Highest point	Official language	Currency	Main exports
Mt Moco, 2620 m	Portuguese	Kwanza	Petroleum, coffee, diamonds
	English, Setswana	Pula	Diamonds, meat, copper
Mt Kartala, 2361 m	French	Franc CFA	Spices
Thabana Ntlenyana, 3482 m	English, Sesotho	Loti	Wool, mohair
Maromo-kotro 2876 m	French, Malagasy	Malgache franc	Coffee, spices
Mt Mlanje, 3000 m	English, Chichewa	Kwacha	Tobacco, tea
Mt Binga, 2436 m	Portuguese	Metical	Fruit, veget-ables, sugar
2483 m	Afrikaans, English	Rand	Diamonds, other minerals, fish
Mount aux Sources, 3299 m	Afrikaans, English	Rand	Gold, diamonds, fruit
Emlembe, 1863 m	English	Lilangeni	Sugar, wood pulp, asbestos
1893 m	English	Kwacha	Copper
Mt Inyangani, 2595 m	English	Zimbabwe dollar	Tobacco

Mozambique

South Africa

Swaziland

Zambia

Zimbabwe

Coal: Important in South Africa, where some of the thickest seams in the world are found. Some coal is turned into petroleum.
Copper: Zambia's main export. The mining area known as the 'Copper Belt' is near the border with Zaire. Small amount in Zimbabwe.
Other minerals: Asbestos (South Africa, Swaziland, Zimbabwe); iron ore (South Africa, Angola); tin (South Africa); zinc (Zaire); oil (Angola).

North America

North America stretches from the bleak Arctic shores of northern Canada and Alaska to the hot, wet jungles of Panama. Three-quarters of the continent is occupied by just two countries: Canada and the USA. The remainder is divided into Mexico and seven other republics of Central America and the many West Indian islands.

The mountain ranges in the west have North America's most spectacular scenery. The rugged Rocky Mountains stretch for nearly 5000 kilometres from Alaska to Mexico. Among other ranges are the Coast Ranges, the Cascades (with the active volcano Mount St Helens), the Sierra Nevada and the Sierra Madre. In the wetter north, snowy peaks overlook waterfalls, gorges, *geysers*, lakes and forests. The *deserts* of the USA and Mexico have salt flats and deep *canyons*.

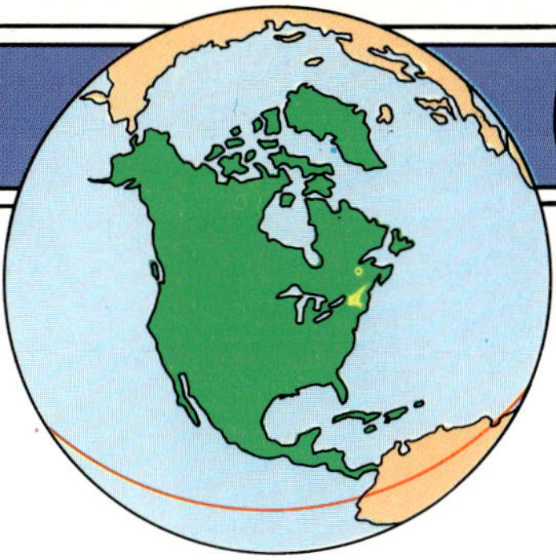

AREA:
24,249,000 sq km (including North and Central America, the West Indies and Greenland).
POPULATION:
382,000,000
INDEPENDENT COUNTRIES:
22
HIGHEST POINT:
Mt McKinley (6194 m) in Alaska.
LOWEST POINT:
Death Valley in California (86 m below sea level).
LARGEST LAKE:
Lake Superior (82,409 sq km).
LONGEST RIVERS:
Mississippi-Missouri-Red Rock (5970 km), Mackenzie-Peace (4240 km).
RICHEST COUNTRIES
(GNP per person – see p. 19):
USA ($11,360), Canada ($10,130).
POOREST COUNTRY:
Haiti ($270)

▲ **Training for American** football in Central Park, New York, USA.

In the USA and Canada, a great *plain* stretches east from the Rockies to the forested Appalachian Mountains and the edge of the old hard rocks forming the Canadian Shield. The mighty Mississippi and its tributaries drain much of this lowland.

The Americas are sometimes called 'the New World' because Europeans only discovered them 500 years ago. Thinking they had reached Asia by sailing west, the first explorers called the natives 'Indians'. Before the Europeans arrived, great empires of the Mayans and Aztecs flourished in Central America; today their ruins are tourist attractions. Most Americans are descended from European settlers: the Spanish came to the West Indies and Central America; the British, French and other Europeans to the USA and Canada.

Canada

ARCTIC OCEAN
QUEEN ELIZABET
MELVILLE I.
BANKS I.
BEAUFORT SEA
VICTORIA ISLAND
Fairbanks
ALASKA (USA)
YUKON TERRITORY
Dawson
Mackenzie Mountains
ROCKY Mountains
Great Bear Lake
Whitehorse
Yukon
Mt Logan 6050m
NORTH WEST TERRITORIES
OCEAN
Mackenzie
Yellowknife
Great Slave Lake
Juneau
Lake Athabasca
Chur
BRITISH COLUMBIA
ALBERTA
SASKATCHEWAN
MANIT
Edmonton
Saskatchewan
PACIFIC
VANCOUVER I.
Calgary
Saskatoon
Lake Winnip
Vancouver
Victoria
Regina
Winnipeg
USA

Canada
Kilometres
0 200 400 600 800
N
0 100 200 300 400 500
Miles
LANDS
BAFFIN BAY
DEVON I.
BAFFIN ISLAND
HUDSON STRAIT
ATLANTIC OCEAN
HUDSON BAY
NEWFOUNDLAND
QUEBEC
Albany
ONTARIO
St John's
PRINCE EDWARD I.
Charlottetown
St. Lawrence
NEW BRUNSWICK
Fredericton
NOVA SCOTIA
Halifax
Lake Nipigon
Lake Superior
Quebec
Trois Rivieres
Montreal
Sudbury
Ottawa
USA
Lake Huron
Lake Michigan
Toronto
Lake Ontario
Niagara Falls
Lake Erie

Canada is the second biggest country in the world, yet there are fewer than 25 million Canadians – an average of only 2·5 people to each square kilometre of land!

Much of Canada is almost empty. Most people live quite close to the southern border, over half near the Great Lakes and St Lawrence River in the Provinces of Quebec and Ontario. This waterway allowed early settlers to travel far into the country, and now canals and locks make it possible for sea-going ships to reach Lake Superior.

Most Canadians live in cities and towns. Toronto and Montreal each have ten per cent of the total population. Montreal was founded by French-speaking settlers and is the largest city in the French-speaking part of Canada.

In the 1880s, there was a rush to the Yukon in search of gold and many small settlements in the north today are mining camps. But in general few people inhabit the vast, cold northern lands and the western mountains. Huge areas of land and many minerals wait to be developed. For this reason Canada is sometimes called the 'country of the future'.

FACTS AND FIGURES

Area: 9,976,130, sq Km
Population: 23,673,000
Capital (population): Ottawa (693,000)
Highest point: Mt Logan, 6050 m
Official languages: English and French
Currency: Dollar
Main exports: Cars and parts, newsprint, wood pulp, oil, natural gas, wheat, iron ore

PRODUCTS

Farming: Only 7% of Canada is cultivated. The prairies in southern Alberta, Saskatchewan and Manitoba are the most important areas for cattle-ranching and growing crops.
Main crops: Wheat (most of which is exported); other cereals (barley, oats, rye) and oil-seeds.
Forestry: About 35% of the land is forested, mostly coniferous trees. Canada is the largest exporter of newsprint in the world.
Fishing: Rich fishing areas near Newfoundland; salmon fishing off Pacific coast. Canada is a major fish exporter.
Minerals: One of the world's major producers of nickel, gold, copper, zinc, silver, lead, natural gas, iron ore, asbestos, uranium, potash.
Industry: Now produces seven times more wealth than agriculture. Great variety of industrial goods, mainly from St Lawrence and Great Lakes area (especially Toronto and Montreal).

▲ **A highway** through the forested Rocky Mountains.

PROVINCES AND TERRITORIES

Province/ Territory	Area (in sq km)	Population	Capital (population)
Alberta	661,187	2,009,000	Edmonton (490,000)
British Columbia	948,559	2,567,000	Victoria (225,000)
Manitoba	650,089	1,030,000	Winnipeg (590,000)
New Brunswick	73,437	701,000	Fredericton (45,300)
Newfoundland	404,518	574,000	St John's (148,000)
North-West Territory	3,379,693	43,000	Yellowknife (8,300)
Nova Scotia	55,491	847,000	Halifax (273,000)
Ontario	1,068,586	8,500,000	Toronto (2,865,000)
Prince Edward Island	5,657	123,000	Charlottetown (19,200)
Quebec	1,540,685	6,299,000	Quebec (559,000)
Saskatchewan	651,902	957,100	Regina (160,000)
Yukon Territory	536,326	22,000	Whitehorse (13,500)

United States of America

CANADA
KEY
CONN. = CONNECTICUT
MASS. = MASSACHUSETTS
N.H. = NEW HAMPSHIRE
★ = a state capital
MAINE
Augusta
VERMONT
N.H.
Boston
CAPE COD
MASS.
Hartford
CONN.
RHODE ISLAND
LONG ISLAND
Albany
New York City
NEW YORK
Lake Ontario
Buffalo
Lake Superior
Lake Michigan
Lake Huron
Lake Erie
MICHIGAN
Lansing
Detroit
MINNESOTA
Minneapolis
St. Paul
WISCONSIN
Mississippi
Madison
Milwaukee
Chicago
IOWA
Des Moines
Omaha
ILLINOIS
Springfield
St. Louis
INDIANA
Indianapolis
OHIO
Columbus
Cleveland
Cincinnati
Ohio
PENNSYLVANIA
Pittsburgh
Harrisburg
Philadelphia
NEW JERSEY
DELAWARE
Baltimore
Washington DC
MARYLAND
WEST VIRGINIA
Charleston
VIRGINIA
Richmond
Appalachian Mountains
KENTUCKY
Frankfort
Kansas City
Topeka
Jefferson City
MISSOURI
Mississippi
TENNESSEE
Nashville
Memphis
Tennessee
NORTH CAROLINA
Raleigh
SOUTH CAROLINA
Columbia
Charleston
Savannah
ARKANSAS
Little Rock
OKLAHOMA
Red
Dallas
MISSISSIPPI
Jackson
ALABAMA
Birmingham
Montgomery
GEORGIA
Atlanta
LOUISIANA
Baton Rouge
New Orleans
Houston
FLORIDA
Tallahassee
Tampa
Miami
ATLANTIC OCEAN
GULF OF MEXICO
Kilometres
0 100 200 300 400 500
Miles 0 100 200 300
N

USA

The United States of America is the fourth largest country in the world, in both area and population. The mainland area is divided into 48 States. Alaska, the 49th State, is a desolate mountainous territory north-west of Canada. The 50th State is Hawaii – 312 warm, wet and mostly volcanic islands in the Pacific Ocean.

Most Americans are descended from European settlers. The first colonists settled on the Atlantic coast, hemmed in by the Appalachian Mountains which were difficult to cross. Gradually, immigrants established farms on the endless flat *plains* of the interior, stretching from the Great Lakes to the Gulf of Mexico, often taking over land used for hunting by American Indians. Explorers and miners travelled west through the Rocky Mountains, facing many hazards in the mountains and *deserts* of the West before reaching the Pacific coast.

Even today, half the population lives in the north-east, where industry is concentrated. The USA is a rich nation, with profitable factories, mines and highly mechanized farms. It uses more energy than any other country in the world. Yet some of its people, including minorities such as the Indians, do not have much share in this wealth.

FACTS AND FIGURES

Area: 9,363,123 sq km
Population: 226,504,825 (at 1980 census)
Capital (population): Washington DC (635,185)
Largest city (population): New York (7,015,608)
Highest point: Mt McKinley, Alaska (6194 m)
Official language: English
Currency: Dollar
Main exports: Machinery, vehicles, cereals, aircraft and parts, chemicals, coal, soya beans, iron and steel goods, textiles, cotton

◀ **The Grand Tetons,** mountains in Wyoming.

▶ **Irish-Americans** celebrate St Patrick's Day in Pittsburgh.

THE AMERICAN PEOPLE

The motto of the USA is *E pluribus unum* – 'out of many, one people'.

European Immigrants and their descendants form 83% of the population. The English first settled the East; the French came to the south (naming New Orleans); the Spanish to the West (founding Los Angeles and San Francisco).

Black Americans form about 12% of the population. They are mostly descendants of slaves brought from West Africa to the southern states to work on *plantations*. After the Civil War of 1861–5, all slaves were freed.

Native Americans (Red Indians) number less than a million. Many were killed when white people took their land.

Other Americans are descended from immigrants from China, Japan, the Philippines, Puerto Rico and Mexico.

AMERICAN CITIES

Most American cities are laid out on a 'gridiron' plan, with roads crossing each other at right angles. The first skyscrapers were built in the USA, on Manhattan Island, New York. Today, the world's tallest office block is in Chicago: the Sears Tower (443 m high, with 110 storeys). The world's tallest block of flats is also in Chicago (197 m high, with 70 storeys).

Nearly eight out of ten Americans live in towns and cities. There are 35 urban areas with more than a million people – though often State capitals are not the largest towns. Few people actually live in the city centres. Instead many live in large suburbs.

The five largest cities with their populations are:
New York City (7,051,608),
Chicago (2,969,570),
Los Angeles (2,950,010),
Philadelphia (1,680,235),
Houston (1,544,992).

CLIMATE AND FARMING

Most of the USA lies south of latitude 49° North. San Francisco and New York are on the same latitude as Madrid and Rome, so it is not surprising that almost all the USA is as hot as southern Europe in summer. The East is humid as well as hot because of tropical winds from the Gulf of Mexico, and there is the risk of *hurricanes*. The south-west is *desert*, with hot, dry air. In winter, much of the USA is very cold and there are heavy snowfalls in the north.

Farming: Nearly half the land is farmed, but only 2% of the working population works in agriculture. The varied climate means a wide range of crops. The Great Plains between Appalachians and Rockies are the richest farmland.

Main crops: Leading producer of soya beans, cotton, fruits, maize (corn), wheat, sugar (cane and beet), tobacco and grapes.

MINERALS AND INDUSTRY

Minerals: Coal is plentiful, especially in Appalachians. Oil mainly from Gulf of Mexico and California. Iron ore from near Lake Superior. Sulphur and phosphates on Gulf Coast. Most other minerals in West. Copper, lead, zinc and uranium important.

Energy: Coal and oil. Also nuclear power (which uses the uranium) and *hydro-electricity.*

Industry: The world's most industrialized nation. Makes 25% of the world's steel (Pennsylvania and Great Lakes area), and 25% of the world's cars (Detroit area); many other engineering industries of all kinds. Also chemicals, textiles, food processing, tobacco, clothing, furniture, newsprint and other timber products.

Service industry: Most people are employed in service industries such as shops, banks, government medical care, education, transport, radio and television, and tourism.

US STATES

State	Capital	Area (in sq km)	Population (1980)
Alabama	Montgomery	133,667	3,890,061
Alaska	Juneau	1,518,800	400,481
Arizona	Phoenix	295,023	2,717,866
Arkansas	Little Rock	137,539	2,285,513
California	Sacramento	411,013	23,668,562
Colorado	Denver	269,998	2,888,834
Connecticut	Hartford	12,973	3,107,576
Delaware	Dover	5,328	595,225
Florida	Tallahassee	151,670	9,739,992
Georgia	Atlanta	152,488	5,464,265
Hawaii	Honolulu	16,705	965,000
Idaho	Boise	216,412	943,935
Illinois	Springfield	146,075	11,418,461
Indiana	Indianapolis	93,993	5,490,179
Iowa	Des Moines	145,790	2,913,387
Kansas	Topeka	213,063	2,363,208
Kentucky	Frankfort	104,623	3,661,433
Louisiana	Baton Rouge	125,674	4,203,972
Maine	Augusta	86,026	1,124,660
Maryland	Annapolis	27,394	4,216,446
Massachusetts	Boston	21,386	5,737,037
Michigan	Lansing	150,779	9,258,344
Minnesota	St Paul	217,735	4,077,148
Mississippi	Jackson	123,584	2,520,638
Missouri	Jefferson City	180,486	4,917,444
Montana	Helena	381,086	786,690
Nebraska	Lincoln	200,017	1,570,006
Nevada	Carson City	286,297	799,184
New Hampshire	Concord	24,097	920,610
New Jersey	Trenton	20,295	7,364,158
New Mexico	Santa Fe	315,113	1,299,968
New York	Albany	128,401	17,557,288
North Carolina	Raleigh	136,197	5,874,429
North Dakota	Bismarck	183,022	652,695
Ohio	Columbus	106,765	10,797,419
Oklahoma	Oklahoma City	181,089	3,025,266
Oregon	Salem	251,180	2,632,663
Pennsylvania	Harrisburg	117,412	11,866,728
Rhode Island	Providence	3,144	947,154
South Carolina	Columbia	80,432	3,119,208
South Dakota	Pierre	199,551	690,178
Tennessee	Nashville	109,411	4,590,750
Texas	Austin	692,402	14,228,383
Utah	Salt Lake City	219,931	1,461,037
Vermont	Montpelier	24,887	511,456
Virginia	Richmond	105,716	5,346,279
Washington	Olympia	176,617	4,130,163
West Virginia	Charleston	62,629	1,949,644
Wisconsin	Madison	145,438	4,705,335
Wyoming	Cheyenne	253,596	470,816

◀ **A modern steel works:** the railway brings iron ore and coal.

Central America and the West Indies

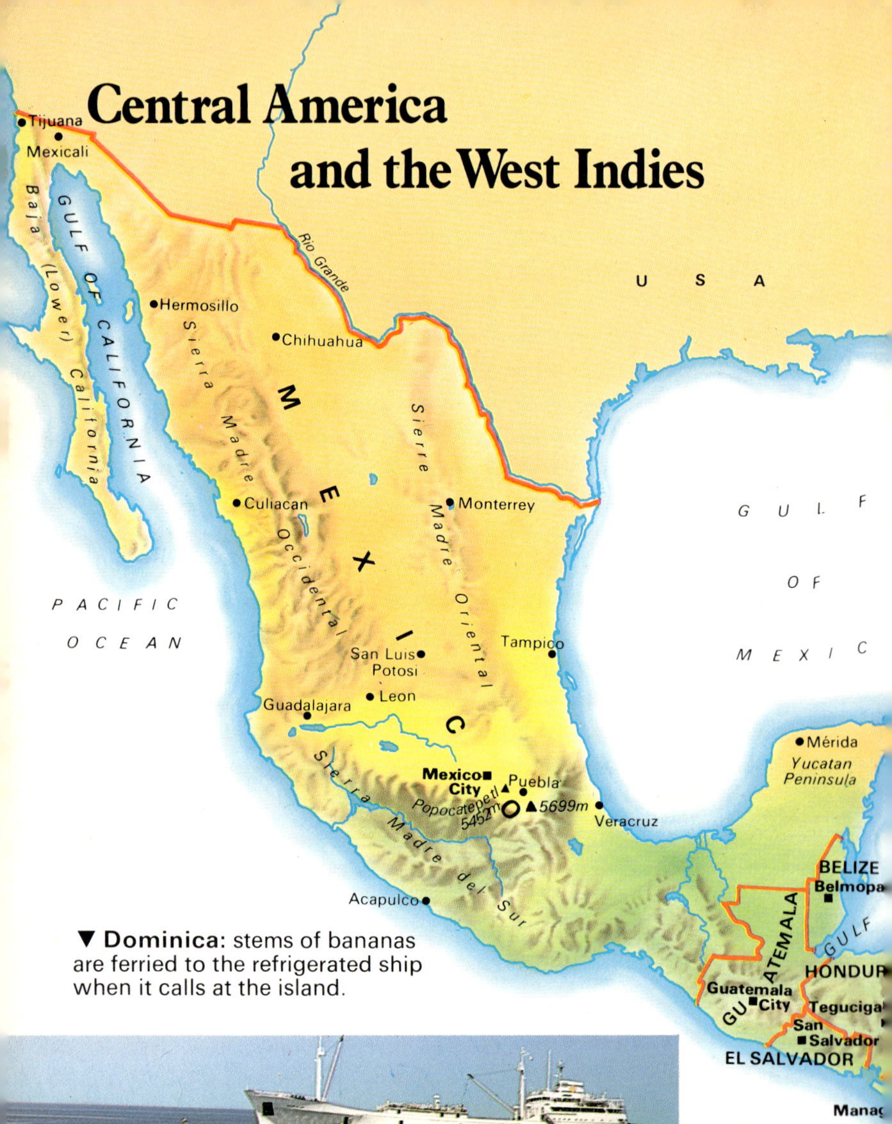

▼ Dominica: stems of bananas are ferried to the refrigerated ship when it calls at the island.

Kilometres
0 200 400 600 800
N
0 100 200 300 400 500
Miles
KEY
BAR. = BARBADOS
GU. = GUADELOUPE (France)
MA. = MARTINIQUE (France)
ST.V. = ST VINCENT & THE GRENADINES
V.I. = VIRGIN ISLANDS (Britain)
ATLANTIC OCEAN
STRAITS OF FLORIDA
Nassau
BAHAMAS
Havana
Santa Clara
CUBA
Cienfuegos
Camaguey
Holguin
Santiago de Cuba
GREATER ANTILLES
HAITI
DOMINICAN REPUBLIC
Port-au-Prince
Santo Domingo
PUERTO RICO
San Juan
ANTIGUA & BARBUDA
ST. KITTS
JAMAICA
Kingston
LEEWARD ISLANDS
GU.
DOMINICA
MA.
ST LUCIA
WINDWARD ISLANDS
BAR.
ST.V.
GRENADA
LESSER ANTILLES
ONDURAS
CARIBBEAN SEA
AGUA
TRINIDAD & TOBAGO
STA RICA
San José
Panama Canal
PANAMA
Panama
VENEZUELA
COLOMBIA

Belize

Costa Rica

El Salvador

Guatemala

Country (Independent)	Area (in sq km)	Population	Capital (population)
BELIZE (1981)	22,965	135,000	Belmopan (4000)
COSTA RICA (1821)	50,700	2,329,000	San José (250,000)
EL SALVADOR (1821)	21,041	4,820,000	San Salvador (682,000
GUATEMALA (1821)	108,889	7,436,000	Guatemala City (1,500,000)
HONDURAS (1821)	112,088	3,941,000	Tegucigalpa (445,000)
MEXICO (1821)	1,972,547	74,539,000	Mexico City (9,618,000)
NICARAGUA (1823)	130,000	2,851,000	Managua (553,000)
PANAMA (1914)	75,650	2,012,000	Panama (467,000)

Mexico and seven small republics are situated on the narrow, mountainous stretch of land between the USA and South America. All these countries, except Belize, are Spanish-speaking and were part of the Spanish Empire until the 1820s. Unlike the USA, these are poor countries, although oil is bringing wealth to Mexico.

Northern Mexico is desert. A high *plateau* between two mountain ranges gradually narrows towards Mexico City and ends in an area of active *volcanoes* which includes Popocatepetl (5452 metres). The mountains – with volcanoes – run south to Panama. Most of Central America is hot, *tropical* jungle, except in the mountains which are cooler. In general the Pacific coast is more developed than the east coast, with many tropical crops grown on large *plantations* for export.

In many of these countries, development has been hindered by revolutions and civil wars. Devastating *earthquakes* have occurred too. While Mexico has a bigger population than any European country, the other republics have fewer people than New York or Greater London.

Official language	Currency	Main exports
English, Spanish	Dollar	Sugar, other food, clothing
Spanish	Colon	Manufactured goods, coffee, bananas
Spanish	Colon	Coffee, cotton
Spanish	Quetzal	Coffee, cotton, bananas, beef
Spanish	Lempira	Bananas, coffee, meat, timber
Spanish	Peso	Manufactured goods, oil, coffee, sugar, cotton
Spanish	Cordoba	Coffee, cotton, meat, chemicals
Spanish	Balboa	Petroleum products, bananas, sugar, shrimps

Honduras

Mexico

Nicaragua

Panama

THE PANAMA CANAL

The Panama Canal (82 km), completed in 1914, is one of the greatest engineering feats in the world – mountains, jungles and diseases had been enormous problems. It opened a route from the Atlantic to the Pacific that saved the long, stormy journey around Cape Horn. It is still the world's busiest ship canal. Part of its course is through Lake Gatun. A series of locks raises the ships to the level of the lake which is 26 m above sea level. This makes the journey slow, and ships have to wait for one-way convoys. There are plans to widen the canal.

The West Indies are beautiful islands in the warm Caribbean Sea. The four larger islands in the west are called the Greater Antilles. The Lesser Antilles are the small *coral* or volcanic islands in the east.

Throughout the West Indies, farming is important. It was to the sugar plantations here that slaves were first brought from West Africa, and sugar is still an important export crop. Several smaller islands now grow bananas as their main crop.

Antigua & Barbuda

Bahamas

Barbados

Cuba

Dominica

Dominican Republic

Grenada

Country (Independent)	Area (in sq km)	Population	Capital (population)
ANTIGUA AND BARBUDA (1981)	442	77,000	St John's (23,500)
BAHAMAS (1973)	13,935	237,000	Nassau (130,000)
BARBADOS (1966)	431	257,000	Bridgetown (88,000)
CUBA (1898)	114,524	10,346,000	Havana (1,735,000)
DOMINICA (1978)	751	82,000	Roseau (17,000)
DOMINICAN REPUBLIC (1844)	48,734	5,776,000	Santo Domingo (818,000)
GRENADA (1974)	344	113,000	St George's (30,000)
HAITI (1804)	27,750	5,220,000	Port-au-Prince (507,000)
JAMAICA (1962)	10,991	2,297,000	Kingston (635,000)
ST LUCIA (1979)	616	130,000	Castries (45,000)
ST VINCENT & THE GRENADINES (1979)	388	113,000	Kingstown (23,000)
TRINIDAD AND TOBAGO (1962)	5130	1,193,000	Port-of-Spain (63,000)

* Trinidad and Tobago is shown on the map on page 149.

There are minerals on the larger islands and industry, though generally small scale, is growing in importance. Tourism is an important money-earner: Americans and others escape from cold winters to the hot sun and palm-fringed beaches. The West Indies are less popular in summer, when it is hot and humid, and *hurricanes* are sometimes devastating. A major problem is providing enough jobs, and many West Indians have gone overseas to find work.

Official language	Currency	Main exports
English	East Caribbean (EC) dollar	Petroleum products
English	Bahamanian dollar	Petroleum products
English	EC dollar	Sugar, petroleum products, electrical goods, clothing
Spanish	Peso	Sugar, tobacco
English	EC dollar	Bananas, citrus fruit
Spanish	Peso	Sugar, coffee
English	EC dollar	Nutmeg, cocoa, bananas
French	Gourde	Coffee, bauxite
English	Jamaican dollar	Alumina and bauxite
English	EC dollar	Bananas
English	EC dollar	Bananas
English	Trinidad dollar	Oil, asphalt, chemicals, food (sugar, fruit, cocoa, coffee)

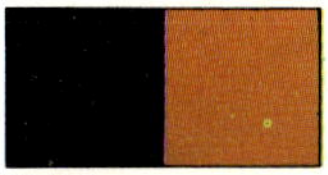
Haiti

Jamaica

St Lucia

St Vincent & Grenadines

Trinidad & Tobago

The following territories are administered by other countries; by UK – Anguilla, Bermuda, British Virgin Islands, Cayman Islands, Monserrat, St Kitts and Nevis, Turks and Caicos Islands; French Overseas Departments – Guadeloupe, Martinique; by Netherlands – Netherlands Antillies; by USA – American Virgin Islands, Puerto Rico.

South America

Almost every type of climate and vegetation in the world is found in South America. The dense *rain forest* of the Amazon lowlands contrasts with the arid Atacama *desert* where almost nothing grows. Most of South America is hot, but the high Andes and the far south are cool for most of the year. South America stretches much further south than Africa or Australasia.

In the early sixteenth century, Spanish 'conquistadors' and Portuguese explorers landed in South America, looking for gold and other riches. Later colonists created huge estates to grow

AREA:
17,600,000 sq Km
POPULATION:
252,000.000
INDEPENDENT COUNTRIES: 12
HIGHEST POINT:
Mt Aconcagua (6960 m).
LONGEST RIVERS:
Amazon (6448 km), Rio de la Plata-Parana (4000 km).
HIGHEST WATERFALL:
Angel Falls (979m), the highest in the world.
LARGEST LAKE:
Titicaca (8300 sq km) in Bolivia and Peru.
RICHEST COUNTRY
(GNP per person – see p. 19):
Venezuela ($3630).
POOREST COUNTRIES:
Bolivia ($570), Guyana ($690).

▶ **An elevated highway** sweeps through the modern city of Caracas, Venezuela.

tropical crops for Europe. The native people, the Amerindians, were driven off the land. Slaves were brought from Africa to work on *plantations* and, later, workers came from Asia. Today many South Americans are of mixed European, Indian and African descent.

The population of South America is increasing rapidly. Cities are growing fast as people move in from the rural areas in the hope of a better life. The city centres have skyscrapers, motorways and superstores, but most newcomers settle in vast shanty towns at the edge of the cities.

▲ **Dressed up** for the annual carnival in Rio de Janeiro, Brazil.

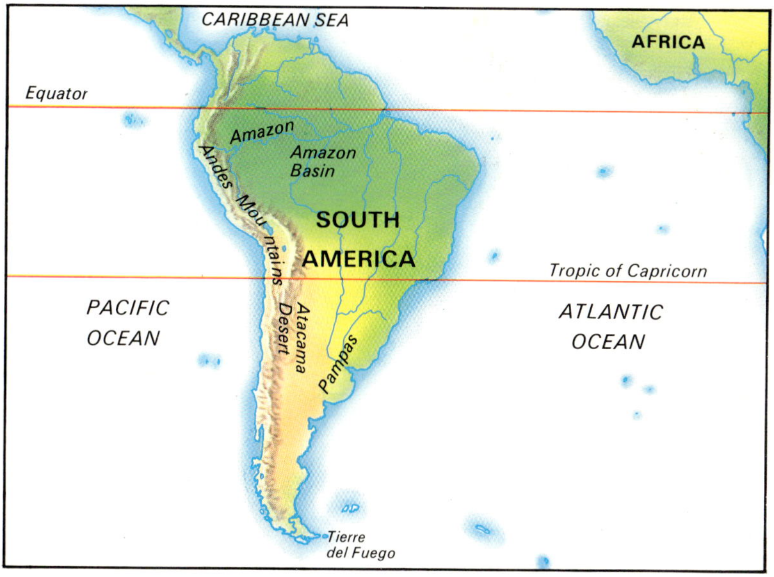

The Andean States

Colombia, Ecuador, Peru and Bolivia are dominated by the Andes mountains. High peaks tower above the forests of the Amazon Basin to the east, the damp coastal lowlands of the north and north-west, and the desert coast of Peru.

Over 800 years ago, the rich Inca civilization developed high in the mountains. Gold and silver attracted the Spaniards who destroyed the Inca empire. Today mineral wealth from the Andes remains important, especially to landlocked Bolivia. In all four countries, Spanish is still the official language.

The mountains divide into several ranges enclosing high *plateaus* where the climate is cool even on the Equator. On the coast of Peru, streams rising in the Andes *irrigate* flourishing, well-populated *oases* and supply water to the coastal towns.

Beyond the high Andean passes are the remote eastern lowlands. The many rivers that feed the Amazon begin in the Andes and rush eastwards through dense *tropical* forest. As transport across the Andes is developed, each country is opening up its Amazon area for new settlers who come to farm the land or work in mining areas.

FACTS AND FIGURES

COLOMBIA
Area: 1,138,914 sq km
Population: 27,966,000
Capital (population): Bogota (3,831,000)
Highest point: Pico Cristobal Colon, 5775 m
Currency: Peso
Main exports: Coffee, emeralds, meat, sugar, oil, hides and skins

ECUADOR
Area: 283,561 sq km
Population: 8,893,000
Capital (population): Quito (560,000)
Highest point: Mt Chimborazo, 6272 m
Currency: Sucre
Main exports: Oil, bananas, cocoa, coffee

PERU
Area: 1,285, 216 sq km
Population: 18,786,000
Capital (population): Lima (3,158,000)
Highest point: Mt Huascaran, 6768 m
Currency: Sol
Main exports: Minerals and metals (silver, lead, zinc, copper), fish and fish-meal, oil

BOLIVIA
Area: 1,093,581 sq km
Population: 5,897,000
Capital (population): Seat of government: La Paz (655,000), Legal capital: Sucre (63,000)
Highest point: Mt Tocoputi, 6755 m
Currency: Peso
Main exports: Tin, oil, natural gas, cotton

CARIBBEAN SEA
5775m
Barranquilla
Cartagena
PANAMA
TRINIDAD
Medellin
Magdalena
Bucaramanga
VENEZUELA
GUYANA
Bogotá
Cali
COLOMBIA
5750 m
Quito
Guayaquil
6272m
ECUADOR
Amazon
Iquitos
Maranon
N
Piura
Andes
Chiclayo
Trujillo
Chimbote
6768 m
Kilometres
0
200
400
600
800
1000
0
200
400
600
Miles
PERU
Mountains
BRAZIL
Callao
Lima
Huancayo
Beni
Cuzco
6384 m
BOLIVIA
El Misti
5822m
Lake
Titicaca
Arequipa
La Paz
Cochabamba
Santa Cruz
Lake
Poopo
Sucre
PARAGUAY
6755m
PACIFIC
CHILE
OCEAN
ARGENTINA
Colombia
Ecuador
Peru
Bolivia

THE NORTHERN ANDES

The western and eastern sides of the Andes have very different vegetation varying with the height above sea level and the rainfall.

Pacific Coast – the West Side: Most people in the area live on this side of the Andes. Farmers work the land or graze animals at all levels except the highest where it snows all year.

Tierra Caliente (tropical zone): The lowest level is hot *desert* and semi desert; *tropical* crops (sugar, bananas and rice) are grown where there is water.

Tierra Templada (temperate zone): Maize, wheat, beans, vegetables and fruit grown here but only cactus scrub survives in the dry parts.

Tierra Fria (cold zone): Grassland for cattle and sheep. Potatoes and wheat grown.

Tierra Helada (freezing zone): Alpine pasture where sheep, llamas, alpacas graze.

Amazon Basin – the East Side: Rainfall is high and the vegetation ranges from grassland and mountain forest down to thick tropical rain forest.

HISTORY

All the north Andean states have Spanish as their official language. The Spaniards conquered the area in the early 16th century. Colombia is named after Christopher Columbus. In the early 19th century, when Spain was weak after the Napoleonic Wars, these countries became independent: Bolivia (1825), Colombia (1819), Ecuador (1822), Peru (1821). Bolivia is named after one of the leaders and heroes of the wars of independence, Simón Bolívar. At independence, however, it was the people of Spanish descent who formed the new governments, not the Indians, who are still the poorest people in these countries.

▼ **A cross-section** of the northern Andes.

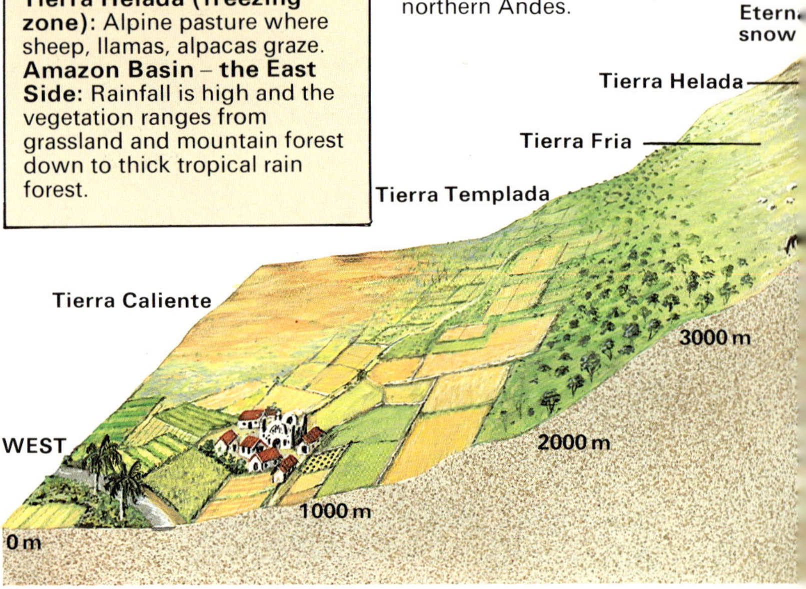

LAKE TITICACA

This is the world's highest navigable lake, shared by Peru and Bolivia, 3811 m above sea level. It can be reached by a spectacular railway from Mollendo, Peru. The lake covers 8300 sq km; its water drains south to Lake Poopo and then disappears into the dry altiplano (high plain). Totoro reeds growing around the shores are used by Indians to make fishing boats. The surrounding area is treeless and bleak, with some coarse grass grazed by llamas and vicunas.

▶ **Indians** in reed boats on Lake Titicaca.

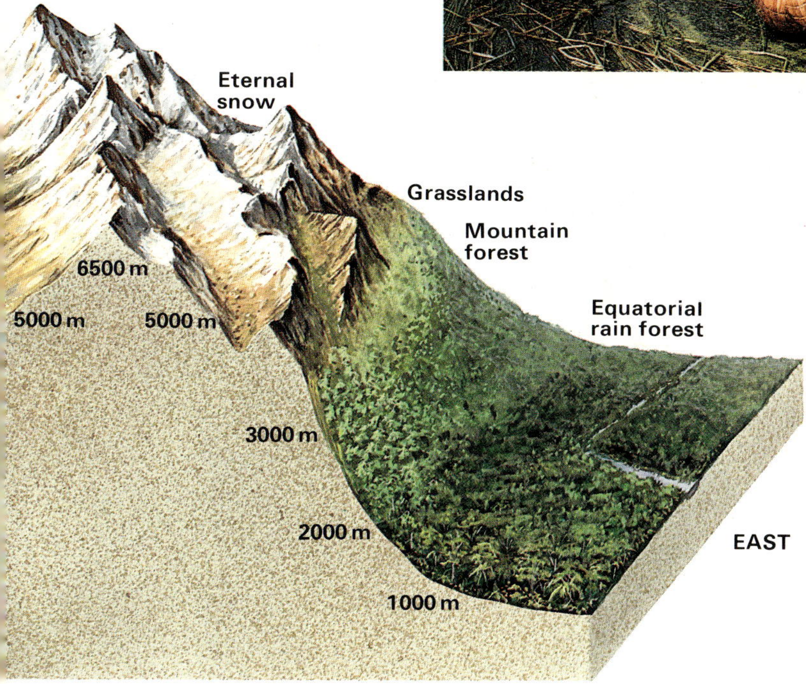

Brazil and its Neighbours

Brazil is the largest country in South America. Most Brazilians live near the Atlantic coast. The biggest cities are in the south: both Rio de Janeiro and Sao Paulo have over five million people. The cities have sky-scrapers, traffic jams and large factory areas. There are rich suburbs but many people live in shanty towns called 'favellas'.

The area around Sao Paulo is famous for its coffee. Brazil grows more coffee than any other country. Sugar cane is another important crop – some is used to make 'gasohol', the fuel used to power Brazilian-made cars. Brazil has plenty of coal, iron ore and other minerals, but no oil.

The north-eastern parts of Brazil are poorer. Rainfall is uncertain, and most of the land is owned by a few rich landlords. In bad years, many tenant farmers are forced to move to the cities of the south or to Amazonia in hope of a better life.

The Brazilian government is building roads into the vast *rain forests* which cover the Amazon lowlands in the north. These rain forests reach into Venezuela and the Guianas. Venezuela is the richest country in South America because of its mineral wealth. Oil is pumped out from beneath Lake Maracaibo and iron ore mined on the Caroni River, a tributary of the Orinoco. The Guianas were once small *colonies* of the British, Dutch and French. Most people live near the coast and many inland forest areas are hardly explored.

Port of Spain
TRINIDAD & TOBAGO
Georgetown
GUYANA
Angel Falls
SURINAM
Paramaribo
Cayenne
FRENCH GUIANA
Guiana Highlands
ATLANTIC OCEAN
N
AMAZONIA
Manaus
Belém
Sao Luis
Fortaleza
Madeira
Tapajos
Xingu
Tocantins
João Pessoa
Recife
Maceió
Sao Francisco
BRAZIL
Mato Grosso
Salvador
Paraguay
Brasília
Goiania
Brazilian Highlands
BOLIVIA
PARAGUAY
Belo Horizonte
2890m
Parana
Rio de Janeiro
Sao Paulo
Santos
Curitiba
ARGENTINA
Uruguay
Porto Alegre
URUGUAY
Kilometres
0 200 400 600 800 1000
Miles 0 200 400 600

Country (language)	Area (in sq km)	Population	Capital (population)	Highest point
BRAZIL (Portuguese)	8,511,965	133,882,000	Brasilia (979,000)	Pico de Bandeira, 2890 m
FRENCH GUIANA (French)	91,000	76,000	Cayenne (36,000)	—
GUYANA (English)	214,000	887,000	Georgetown (183,000)	Mt Roraima, 2810 m
SURINAM (Dutch, English)	163,265	404,000	Paramaribo (152,000)	Julianatop, 1286 m
VENEZUELA (Spanish)	912,050	15,920,000	Caracas (3,508,000)	Pico Bolivar, 5007 m

MINERALS AND POWER

Minerals: Venezuela is one of the world's leading oil producers, with oil pumped from beneath Lake Maracaibo. Its other minerals include iron ore and gold. Bauxite is important in Guyana and Surinam. Guyana also mines diamonds and gold. Brazil exports minerals such as asbestos, chrome, iron ore, manganese and industrial diamonds. It has huge reserves which have not yet been exploited.

Hydro-electricity: The world's largest hydro-electric power scheme, the Itaipu Dam, has been built by Brazil and Paraguay on the mighty Parana River. It generates six times as much power as the Aswan Dam in Egypt. Both countries will benefit from cheap electricity. Hydro-electricity is also being developed on the Caroni River in Venezuela.

EQUATORIAL CLIMATE

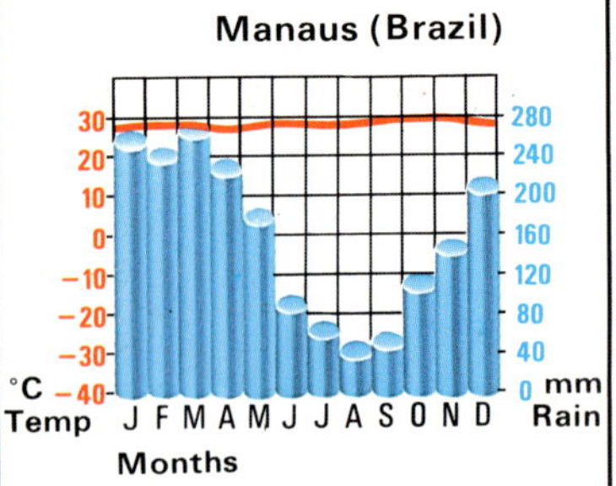

In the rain forests there is plenty of rain every month. Rain storms are expected *every* afternoon for most of the year and it is always hot and damp. Dense forest flourishes, but the soil is not very rich. Once trees are cut down, the soil is easily washed away. The graph shows the temperature and rainfall in Manaus, a port on the Amazon built last century when the rubber trade flourished.

Currency	Main exports
Cruzeiro	Coffee, machinery, vehicles, soya beans, cocoa
French franc	Bananas, shrimps, bauxite
Guyanese dollar	Bauxite and alumina, sugar, rice, timber
Guilder	Bauxite and alumina, rice, citrus fruit
Bolivar	Oil, iron, coffee, cocoa

THE MULTI-STOREY RAIN FOREST

The Amazon rain forest has five main layers as shown in the diagram (right). The layers and their characteristics are:
Emergent layer: A few trees grow high above the others.
Canopy layer: A thick mass of treetops which break the heavy rain into fine spray. Many plants and animals live here on nuts and fruit.
Middle layer: This layer, sometimes called the under-storey, is also dark. Lianas (creepers) and climbing plants grow and young trees struggle towards the light.
Lower layer: Some shrubs and young trees. Tall trees have buttress roots. Dark.
Ground layer: Little light but very damp. Seedlings, herbs and fungi grow in the fragile soil.

The Southern States

A huge statue called 'the Christ of the Andes' stands in a mountain pass between Chile and Argentina, representing peace between these two countries. The boundary between them follows the crest of the Andes. As a result, Chile is a long, thin country squeezed between the Andes and the Pacific. Its maximum width is only 400 kilometres, but it stretches 4300 kilometres from 18° South to Cape Horn, 55° South.

There is far more land between the Andes and the Atlantic Ocean, and Argentina is the second largest country in South America. But it also extends a long way from north to south – from the Tropic of Capricorn to South America's stormy tip on Tierra del Fuego, only 960 kilometres from Antarctica.

Chile and Argentina are mainly *temperate* countries, unlike the rest of South America, which is *tropical.* Although Spain occupied them, they were much less useful than the tropical *colonies* because they produced fewer of the goods that Spain wanted. These countries also had fewer Amerindian inhabitants, so when Chile and Argentina became independent (1810–1818), they were still sparsely populated.

Today most people in these countries are descendants of white settlers and are Spanish-speaking. Immigration from Europe has continued, especially from Italy. The majority of people live in towns, where the contrast in the lives of the rich and the poor is very noticeable. In the rural areas, most of the land is divided into huge estates owned by wealthy people who often live in the cities.

▼ **On the pampas** of Argentina, cattle are rounded up by cowboys called gauchos.

PERU
BOLIVIA
BRAZIL
PARAGUAY
Asunción
Arica
Iquique
Antofagasta
Atacama Desert
Andes Mountains
Gran Chaco
Tucumán
Salado 6885m
Salado
Parana
Uruguay
PACIFIC OCEAN
CHILE
ARGENTINA
San Juan
Córdoba
Santa Fé
Valparaiso
Aconcagua 6960m
Mendoza
Santiago
Rosario
URUGUAY
Buenos Aires
Montevideo
La Plata
Talca
Concepcion
Pampas
Colorado
Bahia Blanca
Mar del Plata
Temuco
Valdivia
Negro
ATLANTIC OCEAN
Puerto Montt
Patagonia
Puerto Deseado
N
FALKLAND ISLANDS (Britain)
Rio Gallegos
Punta Arenas
Tierra del Fuego
Cape Horn
Kilometres
0 200 400 600 800 1000
0 200 400 600
Miles

ARGENTINA
Area: 2,766, 889 sq km
Population: 27,796,000
Capital (population): Buenos Aires (9,677,000)
Highest point: Mt Aconcagua, 6960 m
Official language: Spanish
Currency: Peso
Main exports: Foodstuffs (mainly cereals), tobacco, meat and meat products, textiles, leather, machinery

CHILE
Area: 765,945 sq km
Population: 11,478,000
Capital (population): Santiago (3,692,000)
Highest point: Ojos del Salado, 6885 m
Official language: Spanish
Currency: Peso
Main exports: Copper, paper, wood pulp, timber, iron ore, nitrates

PARAGUAY
Area: 406,752 sq km
Population: 3,254,000
Capital (population): Asuncion (463,000)
Highest point: Cerro Tatug, 700 m
Official language: Spanish
Currency: Guarani
Main exports: Cotton, soya, beans, timber

URUGUAY
Area: 176,216 sq km
Population: 2,934,000
Capital (population): Montevideo (1,230,000)
Highest point: Cerro de las Animas, 500 m
Official language: Spanish
Currency: Peso
Main exports: Meat, wool, hides and skins

EAST OF THE ANDES

The Chaco in Paraguay and northern Argentina has tall grass, thorny trees, and marshland in the rainy season. Mostly undeveloped, but some cotton is grown.

The Pampas (fields) cover most of Uruguay and the richest fifth of Argentina, centred on Buenos Aires. On these flat grasslands, millions of cattle are herded by gauchos (cowboys). Corned beef is a major export. Parts are also farmed for wheat and corn.

Patagonia is the cool, dry area of southern Argentina. The Andes shelter it from the dry westerly winds which have dropped their rain in southern Chile. Few people live in Patagonia: some are descendants of Welsh sheep farmers who still speak Welsh. Sheep-grazing is the main activity, though oil from Patagonia is piped to the towns of the Pampas.

LOS ANDES

The world's longest mountain range, stretching over 7000 km from Venezuela to southern Chile. They are *fold mountains*, with many volcanoes such as El Misti (5822 m) in Peru, and Ojos del Salado (6885 m) in Chile, the world's highest active volcano. *Earthquakes* are common and have caused much damage. Earth movements occur because the floor of the Pacific Ocean is being dragged very, very slowly underneath the continent of South America. There are only a few passes across the Andes and just two spectacular railway routes from Chile to Argentina.

THE THREE CHILES

Northern Chile is *desert.* The driest place on earth is in the Atacama Desert, where there was no rain at all for over 400 years until a freak storm in 1971. But in some parts, rivers from the Andes bring water for *irrigation* and to mining camps. Copper, Chile's main export, comes from the Andes. Nitrates are quarried for fertiliser. **Central Chile** has a *Mediterranean climate.* Most people, towns, industry and farms are in this part. Fruit, vines and other crops are grown. **Southern Chile** is cool, remote and mountainous. There are forests, islands and deep fiords, but few people.

Argentina

Chile

Paraguay

Uruguay

▼ **Mt Aconcagua,** highest point in the Andes, on the Chile-Argentine border.

▼ **The Atacama Desert** in northern Chile, the driest place on Earth.

Australasia

Australia, New Zealand and thousands of islands in the vast Pacific Ocean make up Australasia. Papua-New Guinea shares an island with the Asian country of Indonesia – a reminder that Australasia and Asia are next-door neighbours.

Distances are huge in Australasia. The Pacific Ocean is the world's largest. From Western Australia to Pitcairn Island is about 12,000 kilometres and from Stewart Island, New Zealand to Wake Island is about 7500 kilometres. But in this vast ocean, land areas are small. Most of the countries of Australasia are groups of tiny islands. The only large land area is Australia – sometimes classed as the smallest continent or the largest island in the world.

The total population of Australasia is smaller than that of any other continent except Antarctica. But the amount of habitable land is small. Many islands are *volcanoes* or bare *coral,* or are true desert islands because of low rainfall. Australia itself is mostly *desert*.

Just over half the total population of Australasia lives in

AREA:
8,510,000 sq km (95% of this is Australia and New Zealand).
POPULATION: 24,500,000
INDEPENDENT COUNTRIES: 11
HIGHEST POINT:
Mt Wilhelm (4694 m) in Papua New Guinea.
LOWEST POINT:
Lake Eyre (12 m below sea level) in Australia.
LONGEST RIVERS:
Murray (2575 km) and its tributary, the Darling (2740 km).
RICHEST COUNTRY
(GNP per person – see p. 19):
Australia ($9800)
POOREST COUNTRIES:
Solomon Islands ($460), Tonga ($460).

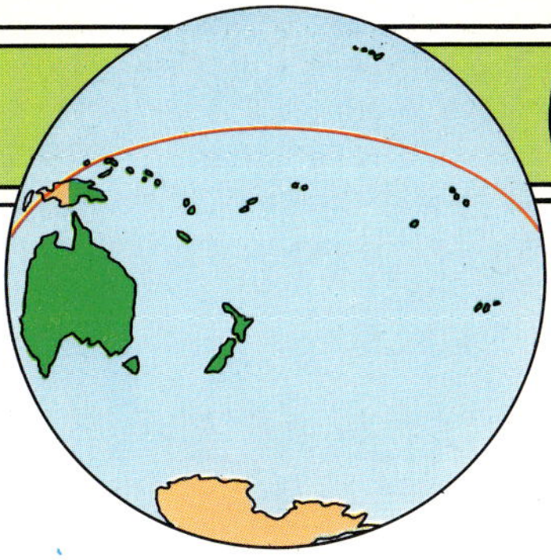

Australia and more than half are descended from European settlers – the majority from Britain. Skilled emigrants from Europe are still encouraged to come to New Zealand and Australia and the native populations of Maoris and Aborigines are now small minorities.

The smaller islands are often grouped according to the people that live on them. These groups are Melanesia, Micronesia and Polynesia. Many of the islands were ruled by Britain, or by other European countries or the USA. Some are now independent.

▲ **A coral reef** around a volcanic island in the Pacific.

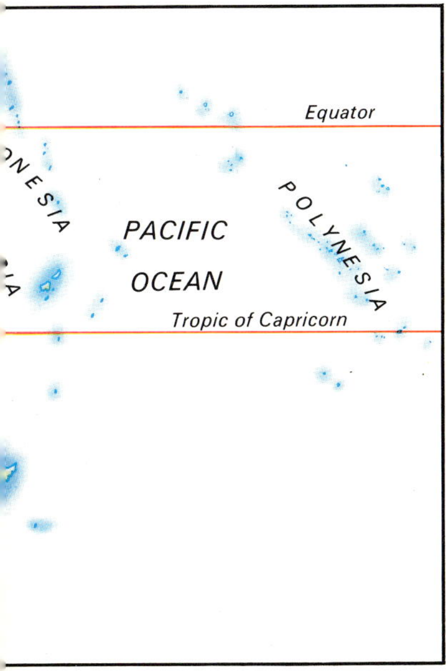

▼ **Sydney Opera House, Australia.** Sydney is Australia's largest city.

The Pacific Islands

The Pacific – meaning 'peaceful' – is a huge ocean. Most of the countries of the Pacific are large groups of tiny islands scattered over thousands of square kilometres of ocean. Even Papua-New Guinea, the largest country, consists of part of one large and mountainous island and more than 600 smaller islands. Yet one of these small islands – Bougainville – has copper mines which provide Papua-New Guinea's main export.

Phosphates are mined on Nauru, but few other islands have mineral resources. On many of the smallest inhabited islands the people are *subsistence farmers*, growing only enough for their own needs. The main *cash crop* throughout the Pacific is coconuts – grown for copra (dried coconut). Other money-earners are sugar, tropical fruit (especially bananas and pineapples), fish, timber, tourism and even postage stamps.

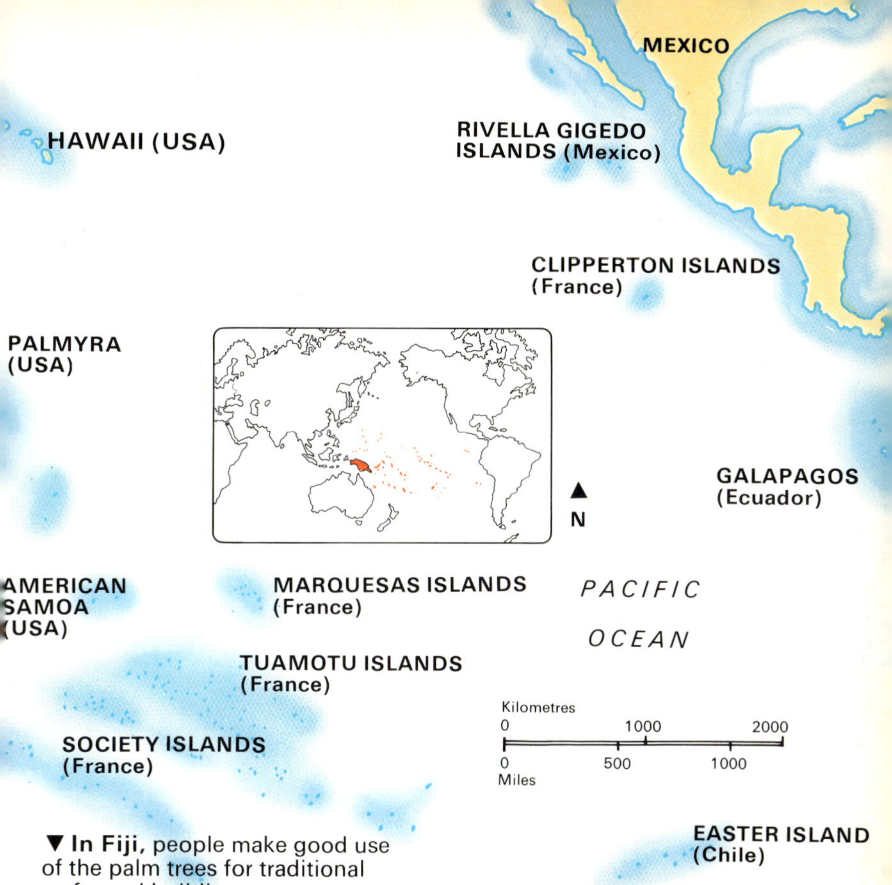

▼ **In Fiji,** people make good use of the palm trees for traditional crafts and buildings.

Fiji

Kiribati

Nauru

Papua-New Guinea

Solomon Islands

Country (Independent)	Inhabited islands	Area (in sq km)	Population
FIJI (1970)	About 100	18,274	656,000
KIRIBATI formerly Gilbert Islands (1979)	21	931	60,000
NAURU (1968)	1	21	7250
PAPUA-NEW GUINEA (1975)	Over 600	461,691	3,221,000
SOLOMON ISLANDS (1978)	6	28,446	242,000
TONGA or Friendly Islands (1970)	169	699	99,000
TUVALU formerly Ellice Islands (1978)	8	25	7349
VANUATU formerly New Hebrides (1980)	Over 80	14,763	113,000
WESTERN SAMOA (1962)	9	2842	164,000

THE DATE LINE

The flight from Fiji to Samoa takes 2 hours. But if you leave Fiji at 2 pm Wednesday you arrive in Samoa at 5 pm on Tuesday! This is because you cross the International Date Line. At 2 am on Wednesday it will be dark in London – at 0° longitude. East from London, for every 15° of longitude, the time will be 1 hour *ahead* (see page 25). In Bangladesh, at 90°E it will be 8 am (6 hours ahead). In Fiji, at 180°E it will be 2 pm.

West from London, for every 15° of longitude, the time will be 1 hour earlier. So when it is 2 am, Wednesday morning in London, in Chicago (90°W) it will be 6 hours earlier, that is 8 pm Tuesday. And in Samoa, 170°W, time is 11 hours behind London, so it is 3 pm Tuesday.

So when you board your flight in Fiji at 2 pm Wednesday, at that very moment in Samoa it is 3 pm Tuesday. Now work out the return flight – if you leave Samoa at 3 pm on Friday, when will you reach Fiji?*

*4 pm Saturday.

Capital (population)	Language	Currency	Main exports
Suva (64,000)	English, Fijian	Fiji dollar	Sugar, coconut oil
Tarawa (20,000)	English, Gilbertese	Australian dollar	Copra
Nauru	English, Nauruan	Australian dollar	Phosphates
Port Moresby (122,000)	English	Kina	Copper, coffee, cocoa, copra
Honiara (15,000)	English	Soloman Is. dollar	Copra, timber, palm oil
Nuku'alofa (18,000)	English	Pa'anga	Copra, bananas
Fongafale (2000)	English, Tuvalu	Australian dollar	Copra
Port Vila (14,000)	French, English, Bislama	Vatu	Copra, fish
Apia (33,000)	English, Samoan	Tala	Bananas, cocoa, copra

Tonga

Tuvalu

Vanuatu

Western Samoa

▼ **Lava flows** from a volcano on one of the Hawaiian Islands.

New Zealand

New Zealand is an isolated country, 2000 kilometres south-east of Australia and 10,000 kilometres west of Chile. It does not have a long history. The first settlers probably arrived only about 1000 years ago. The first European to see the islands was Abel Tasman in 1642, who named it after part of the Netherlands. Captain Cook mapped the coast in 1769.

After about 1840, many people from Britain, and some from other European countries, took over land from the Maoris and settled. They found a country that was pleasantly like the British Isles, but warmer and greener. At first the hills were covered in forests but many trees were felled by the Europeans. Timber was the main building material and a valuable export. The cleared land was used for pastoral farming – which became very important once refrigerated ships made it possible to export perishable goods like meat and dairy produce.

The population is still small, and sixty two per cent of the people live in towns. The largest city is Auckland, which is also the main port, airport and industrial centre. It was the capital until 1865 when this moved to a more central location at Wellington. The main industrial city in South Island is Christchurch.

▼ **Steam from geysers** in North Island is piped to a geo-thermal power station to generate electricity.

Kilometres
0 100 200 300 400
0 50 100 150 200 250
Miles
N
TASMAN
SEA
NEW ZEALAND
Auckland
Hamilton
Rotorua
Lake
Taupo
Gisbourne
New
Plymouth
Egmont
2516m
Napier
Wanganui
NORTH
ISLAND
Palmerston
Nelson
Wellington
Cook
3764m
Southern Alps
Christchurch
Canterbury Plains
PACIFIC
OCEAN
SOUTH
ISLAND
Dunedin
Invercargill
STEWART
ISLAND
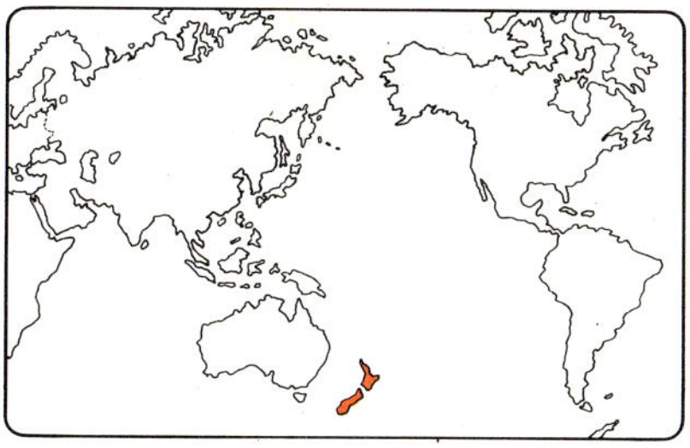

FACTS AND FIGURES

Area: 268, 676 sq km
North Island: 114,681 sq km
South Island: 150,452 sq km
Stewart Island: 1735 sq km
Population: 3,400,000
Independent: 1947
Capital (population): Wellington (350,000)
Largest town (population): Auckland (806,000)
Highest point: Mt Cook, 3764 m
Official language: English
Currency: New Zealand dollar
Main exports: Meat, wool, dairy products, fruit

NATURAL FEATURES

North Island: A volcanic *plateau* lies in the centre of the island, surrounding Lake Taupo. There are many volcanoes – some still active. *Geysers*, boiling mud pools, hot springs, and even hot-water beaches are features of the volcanic activity. Some steam is used in geothermal power stations to produce electricity. There are still vast areas of native bush in the island, where much of the vegetation and wildlife are unique to New Zealand.

South Island: A great range of mountains called the Southern Alps stretches the length of the island, mainly on the west side. The highest point is Mt Cook (3764 m). There are many *glaciers* and lakes, and in the far south the coast is broken by *fiords*. The beautiful scenery attracts tourists and skiers. Some fast-flowing rivers are used to generate *hydro-electricity*. The flat and fertile Canterbury Plains stretch from the Southern Alps to the east coast.

▲ **Beautiful woodcarving** on a Maori meeting hall.

◀ **Mustering sheep** in South Island. The red wool-shearing sheds are sheltered by trees.

THE MAORIS

The Maoris began to arrive in New Zealand about 600 years ago. They came from Polynesia by canoe and first settled in the north. Gradually they moved south. Today Maoris make up 8% of New Zealand's population. Most of them still live in the northern part of North Island, but many now live in cities, especially Auckland. Maori culture, language and music play an important part in New Zealand life. Maori meeting-halls have very fine wood-carvings.

FARMING

New Zealand is the world's largest exporter of lamb and dairy produce, and the second largest exporter of wool. These items account for 80% of the country's exports, yet only 10% of the people work in farming.
Pastoral farming: Very productive animal farming is possible because the grass is excellent and animals can be outdoors all year. About 22,000 dairy farms produce 6 billion litres of milk a year, mainly in the North Island. Much of it is used for butter and cheese.

About 40,000 sheep farmers own about 80 million sheep. The main sheep-farming areas are on South Island – around Christchurch and in the far south.
Arable farming: Important in many areas. New Zealand apples and other fruit such as kiwi fruit are exported.

Australia

MELVILLE I.
Darwin
TIMOR SEA
Arnhem Land
Daly
Wyndham
Ord
Victoria
Broome
Great Sandy Desert
NORTHERN TERRITORY
Mt Bruce 1227 m
Macdonnell R
1524 m
Ashburton
Gibson Desert
Carnarvon
Gascoyne
Ayers Ro
867 m
Murchison
Musgrave Rang
WESTERN AUSTRALIA
Great Victoria Desert
Geraldton
SOU
Kalgoorlie
Nullarbor Plain
INDIAN OCEAN
Perth
Fremantle
Darling Range
GREAT AUSTRALIAN BIGHT
Albany
N
Kilometres
0 200 400 600
0 100 200 300
Miles

ARAFURA SEA
GULF OF CARPENTARIA
GROOTE EYLANDT
WELLESLEY IS.
Cape York Pensinsula
GREAT BARRIER REEF
PACIFIC OCEAN
Mitchell
Cairns
CORAL SEA
Leichhardt
Flinders
Georgina
Townsville
Mount Isa
Great Dividing Range
Rockhampton
ice Springs
QUEENSLAND
Diamantina
Simpson Desert
Brisbane
Toowoomba
Gold Coast
Lake Eyre
Cooper
STRALIA
Darling
Bourke
Lake Torrens
Port Augusta
Whyalla
Flinders Ranges
Broken Hill
NEW SOUTH WALES
Newcastle
Sydney
Wollongong
Murrumbidgee
Adelaide
Wagga Wagga
Canberra
Murray
KANGAROO I.
VICTORIA
Kosciusko 2228m
Australian Alps
Bendigo
Ballarat
Melbourne
Geelong
TASMAN SEA
KING I.
BASS STRAIT
FLINDERS I.
Launceston
TASMANIA
Hobart

Terra Australis Incognita, unknown Southern Land, were the Latin words written across maps until the late 18th century. Only then was the coast of Australia mapped – first by Captain Cook and then by others. At that time, the land was inhabited by small tribes of hunters, called Aborigines by the white settlers. Today, most Australians are descended from immigrants from Europe.

The total population is still small. Two out of every three Australians live in the five big State capital cities, or their suburbs. All these cities are on the coast. The rest of the people are scattered across an enormous area, in small townships, on farms or in mining settlements.

In the east, the Great Dividing Range separates the green lowlands of the east coast from the much drier west. Inland is the outback – a broad lowland area with grazing for sheep and cattle, and good farmland in places where irrigation is possible. Further west is the vast dry *plateau* of the *desert* – the 'dead heart of Australia'.

FARMING

Only 8% of the land can be cultivated or intensively grazed. Much land is rough grazing. Only 6% of the working people are employed in farming.
Sheep: About 140 million. Merino sheep kept in dry areas for wool. Sheep stations are huge, especially on desert edge. The north is too hot for sheep.
Cattle: About 26 million. Dairying in south-east and near main towns. Queensland is chief beef-cattle state, with huge cattle stations.
Main crops: Wheat is the main cereal crop and an important export. Fruit is important in south: peaches and apricots (Murray Valley); pears (Victoria); apples (Tasmania); grapes for wine and sultanas (South Australia). Much fruit is canned and exported.

FACTS AND FIGURES

Official name: The Commonwealth of Australia
Area: 7,686,849 sq km
Population: 15,066,000 (about 100,000 are Aborigines)
Capital (population): Canberra (241,000)
Largest town (population): Sydney (3,193,000)
Highest point: Mt Kosciusko (2228 m) in the Australian Alps
Official language: English
Main exports: Cereals, meat, other foodstuffs such as fruit, sugar, honey; metals and mineral ores, wool
Currency: Australian dollar

▶ **Aborigines** use traditional designs on craft goods which they sell to tourists. They are descended from Australia's original inhabitants.

STATES AND TERRITORIES OF AUSTRALIA

State or territory	Area (in sq km)	Population	Capital (population)
Capital Territory	2,432	247,200	Canberra (241,000)
New South Wales	801,428	5,269,800	Sydney (3,193,000)
Northern Territory	1,347,519	126,300	Darwin (50,000)
Queensland	1,727,522	2,386,000	Brisbane (1,015,000)
South Australia	984,377	1,325,000	Adelaide (933,000)
Tasmania	68,322	428,000	Hobart (168,000)
Victoria	227,618	3,970,000	Melbourne (2,740,00)
Western Australia	2,527,621	1,257,000	Perth (884,000)

ANIMALS AND PLANTS

The continent has been cut off from others for at least 50 million years, and unique plants and animals have developed.
Animals: The best-known are the marsupials – animals whose young are born undeveloped and reared in a pouch, like the kangaroo, the wallaby, the koala, and various marsupial cats, rats and mice. Egg-laying mammals also exist, such as the duck-billed platypus and the spiny ant-eater.
Trees: Eucalyptus (Gum-tree) is the best-known native tree. Forests are mainly in the east and south-east. Felled for wood and paper, eucalyptus is now planted in many dry parts of the world. It burns well so fires are a great danger.

◀ **A koala** snoozing in a eucalyptus tree in eastern Australia.

WATER

Australia is the world's driest continent.
Rain: 70% of the land has less than 50 centimetres of rain a year on average.
Rivers: Most are short and many only flow after heavy rain. The Murray, Darling and Murrumbidgee receive water from highlands in the wetter east.
Lakes: Largest on map is Lake Eyre – usually a salt flat, but occasionally flooded.
Underground water: Important inland. Water from the Great Dividing Range seeps through porous rocks underground and can be tapped by wells and pumps in the outback. It is often called artesian water.
Irrigation: This is vital for much farming. Over 60% along river Murray and tributaries. The Snowy Mountain Scheme (in the Australian Alps) diverts the east-flowing rivers through tunnels to make hydro-electric power and provide water for *irrigation* west of the mountains.

MINERALS

The Eastern Highlands have many minerals, but the main recent finds are in Western Australia.

Gold: Sixth largest producer in world. The gold rushes of the 1850s and 1880s boosted the population. Mined at Kalgoorlie, Broken Hill and elsewhere in north and west.

Iron ore: Now most important mineral and biggest mineral export. Large deposits in west (Mount Bruce area). Basis of iron and steel industry, cars, shipbuilding, and many other industries.

Coal: In east, supplies industry.

Bauxite: World's largest producer. Large deposits in Perth area.

Other minerals: Lead and zinc (Broken Hill, Mt Isa), thorium, uranium (Northern Territory), opals, manganese, nickel and copper.

Oil and gas: From Bass Strait, supply 70% of needs.

▲ **A huge open-cast mine** for iron ore in Western Australia.

▼ **A busy sheep station** in Queensland, Australia.

Antarctica

This cold and desolate continent has the South Pole at its centre. It holds world records for the coldest place, the windiest place, the longest *glacier* and the thickest ice!

Little snow falls so Antarctica is a cold desert, but blizzards are a great hazard. The land area is a vast dome of ice; the sea is a mass of pack-ice and icebergs for most of the year.

Antarctica is a dangerous continent, and no one lives there permanently. About a thousand scientists live in research stations belonging to nine countries. Everything they need has to be brought in by ice-breakers during the short summer, and rubbish has to be taken away. The Antarctic Treaty guarantees the free use of the continent for peaceful purposes only.

▼ **A scientist** in Antarctica measuring the movement of glacier ice.

FACTS AND FIGURES

Area: 13,209,000 sq km (the 5th largest continent)
Population: No permanent inhabitants
Settlement: Research stations owned by Argentina, Australia, France, Japan, New Zealand, South Africa, USSR, UK, USA
Highest point: 5139 m in Vinson Massif
Thickest ice: 4776 m on Wilkes Land. The ice sheet is the largest in the world and contains 90% of the world's ice
South Pole: First reached by Roald Amundsen in December, 1910
Distances to other continents: South America, 960 km; Australia, 2700 km; Africa, 4000 km
Wildlife: No land animals. Seals, whales, penguins, gulls, petrels
Minerals: Known but too expensive to exploit

▲ **Antarctic** wild-life.

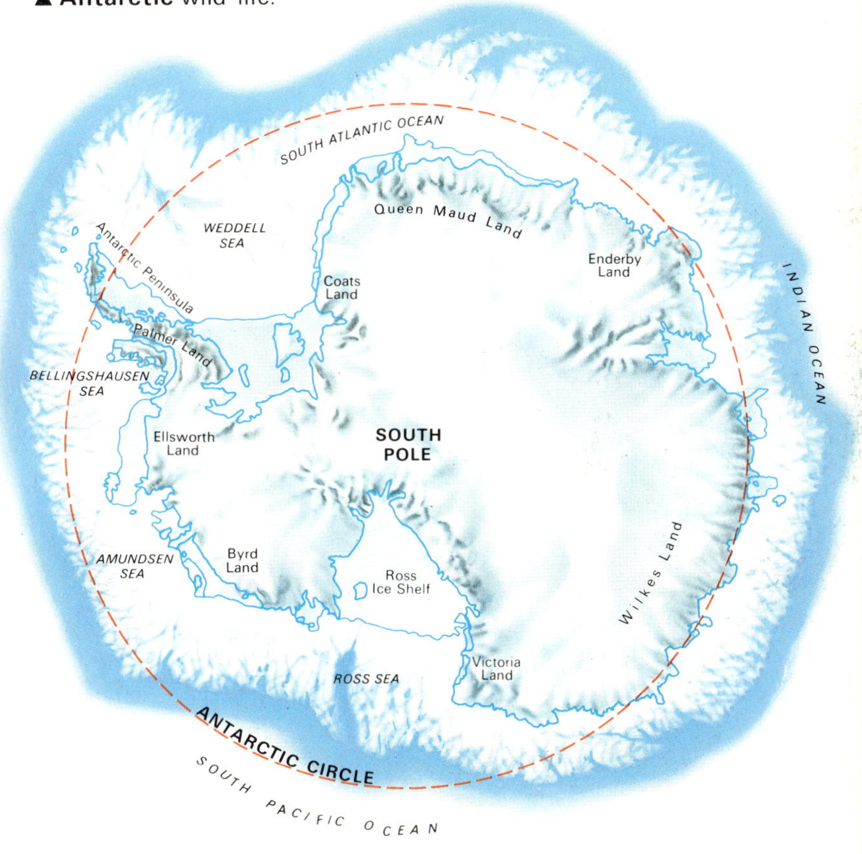

The Arctic

The Arctic is a large ocean surrounded by many islands and by the northern coasts of Norway, USSR, Alaska and Canada. The largest island, Greenland, is covered with an *ice sheet* up to 3000 metres thick. *Glaciers* reach the coast and break up into icebergs.

Few people live in these cold lands, and only a small number of them are Inuit (Eskimoes). A few Eskimoes still build igloos and hunt and fish for their food, but most live in wooden houses and are more likely to travel by motor skidoo than sledge. The majority of people are Americans, Canadians, Danes and Russians who have moved to the Arctic to work on military bases, meteorological stations or in mining camps. The area is rich in minerals: oil in Alaska; iron ore in Canada; nickel, copper and coal in USSR; coal on Spitzbergen; and, in Greenland, the world's only source of cryolite – an aluminium ore.

ARCTIC CLIMATE

Temperatures creep above freezing in only four months of the year, when there is sunshine for up to 24 hours. There is litte rain, but when the winter snow and the topsoil thaw, the *tundra* is a mass of lakes and marsh. Mosses, lichen and dwarf plants flourish for a few weeks – and so do mosquitoes. Caribou, bears and wolves may migrate here from the forests further south. In the cold, dark winter, they leave the treeless landscape to the polar bears, Arctic foxes, seals and walruses.

Svalbard

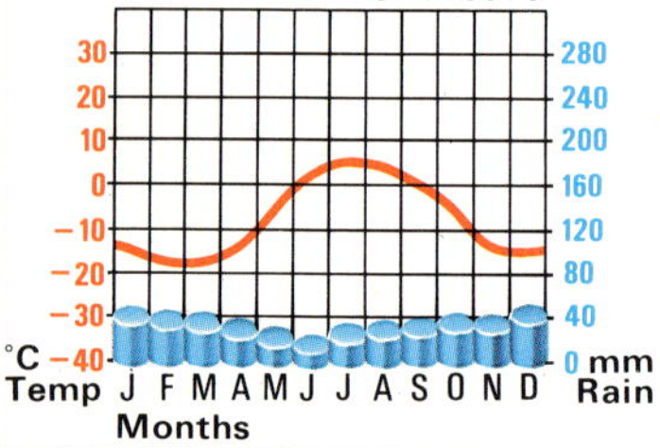

FACTS AND FIGURES

THE ARCTIC
Area of Arctic Ocean: 14,200,000 sq km

North Pole: First reached by Robert Peary in 1909

GREENLAND
Status: Self-governing Danish county
Official name: Kalaatdlit Nunaat
Area: 2,175,600 sq km
Population: 50,000
Capital (population): Godthaab (9000)
Highest point: Mt Forel (3360 m)
Official languages: Danish, Greenlandic
Currency: Danish Krone
Main exports: Fish, cryolite, skins

▶ **At midsummer** in the Arctic you can still see the sun at midnight in the northern sky. It does not set below the horizon.

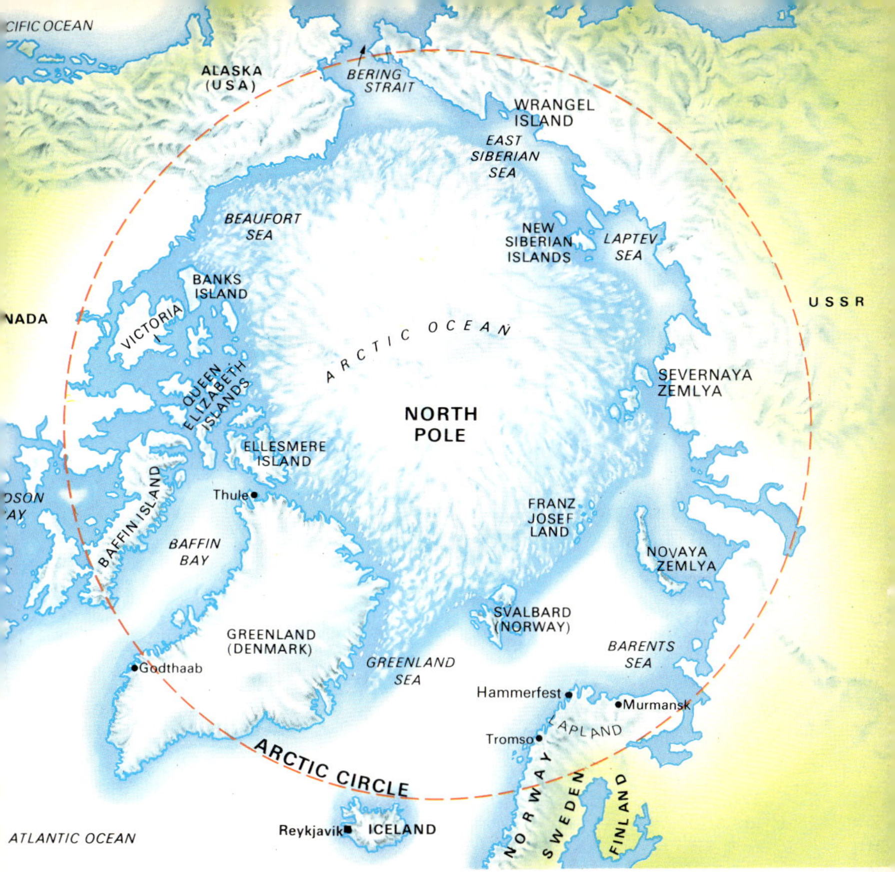
CIFIC OCEAN
ALASKA (USA)
BERING STRAIT
WRANGEL ISLAND
EAST SIBERIAN SEA
BEAUFORT SEA
NEW SIBERIAN ISLANDS
LAPTEV SEA
BANKS ISLAND
USSR
NADA
VICTORIA I.
ARCTIC OCEAN
SEVERNAYA ZEMLYA
QUEEN ELIZABETH ISLANDS
NORTH POLE
ELLESMERE ISLAND
Thule
DSON AY
BAFFIN ISLAND
FRANZ JOSEF LAND
BAFFIN BAY
NOVAYA ZEMLYA
SVALBARD (NORWAY)
GREENLAND (DENMARK)
BARENTS SEA
Godthaab
GREENLAND SEA
Hammerfest
Murmansk
LAPLAND
Tromso
ARCTIC CIRCLE
NORWAY
SWEDEN
FINLAND
Reykjavik
ICELAND
ATLANTIC OCEAN

8 pm
9 pm
10 pm
11 pm
Midnight
1 am
2 am
3 am
4 am

Glossary

Words in *italics* refer to further entries in the glossary.

Agriculture Cultivating the land to grow crops. Sometimes the word is used for pastoral farming (keeping animals) as well as arable farming (growing crops).
Atmosphere The layer of moving air which surrounds the Earth. It consists of nitrogen, oxygen, water vapour and other gases. The atmosphere is concentrated near the Earth's surface, and gets thinner away from the Earth.
Axis An imaginary straight line around which a spinning object rotates. The Earth's axis goes from the North Pole, through the centre of the Earth, to the South Pole. The Earth travels round the Sun, and its axis is tilted in relation to the path of the Earth's orbit (see page 180).
Canyon A deep, steep-sided valley, usually cut by a river in a *desert* area where the sides do not get very worn away by rain-water and streams. The most famous is the Grand Canyon, on the Colorado River, USA, which is over 1600 m deep in parts.
Cash Crops Crops grown mainly for sale and not for the farmer's own food supply. They may include food crops, for example, wheat from the Canadian Prairies. Many have to be processed in factories, for example, sugar cane, cocoa, rubber.
Climate The average weather conditions of a place. Climate figures are averages of figures collected over a number of years (usually at least 30 years), so extremes of heat and cold, drought and flood are hidden. The temperature and rainfall graphs in this atlas help to show what the climate of each place is like.
Colony Usually a country that has been settled by people who have moved far away from their native land, and is now governed by the settlers' home country. The Falkland Islands are a British colony with a Governor sent from the UK.
COMECON Council for Mutual Economic Assistance. Established 1949. Members are Bulgaria, Czechoslovakia, East Germany, Hungary, Poland, Romania, USSR, Yugoslavia (associate member). Cuba, Mongolia and Vietnam are non-European members.
Coral Coral is made by tiny creatures called coral polyps which live in warm sunny seas. When they die, their skeletons join together to form coral reefs and islands.
Core The inner part of the Earth (see page 10).
Crust The outer layer of the Earth (see page 10).
Current (in ocean or sea) A flow of water, usually of similar temperature, across part of an ocean, sea or large lake. Currents at the surface of an ocean are usually caused by winds. An example is the Warm Gulf Stream (becoming the North Atlantic Drift) in the Atlantic.
Delta The Greek letter Δ (delta), used to describe an area of sediments deposited at the mouth of some rivers. Deltas occur when a river brings more alluvia (sand and mud) than sea or lake currents can carry away. Rivers with large deltas include the Nile (page 110) and the Ganges (page 92).
Desert A dry area where little grows. Sometimes defined as an area with less than 250 millimetres of rain a year on average. Bahrain is an example of a place with a desert climate (page 103); the Sahara is the largest desert (page 110); the Atacama is the driest (page 154).
Dunes Mounds or ridges of sand. They are found on some sandy coasts and in sandy *deserts*. Sand dunes move when strong winds blow sand up the side of the dune facing the wind, and the grains roll down

the sheltered side. Sometimes dunes can be 'fixed' by planting special grasses or trees.
Dyke This word can mean four different things: 1. A bank or wall to hold back flood water or the sea (such as dykes built round *polders* in the Netherlands). 2. A ditch for draining land. 3. A man-made ditch built to defend an area (for example Offa's Dyke along the boundary of England and Wales). 4. A wall of solidified volcanic lava formed when the edge of a layer of lava sticks out of the ground.
Earthquake A sudden movement within the Earth's *crust* which causes shock waves which make the Earth's surface shake. Earthquake tremors are recorded on a seismograph.
EEC European Economic Community or Common Market. Established 1957. Members are Belgium, Denmark, France, Greece, Ireland, Italy, Luxembourg, Netherlands, United Kingdom, West Germany.
EFTA European Free Trade Area. Established 1961. Members are Austria, Iceland, Norway, Portugal, Sweden, Switzerland, Finland (associate member).
Estuary The mouth of a river where it enters the sea. Usually it is much wider than the rest of the river. An estuary has tides so river water and sea water mix.
Fiord (Fjord) A long, steep-sided inlet of the sea in a mountainous coastal area. Originally it was a valley eroded by a *glacier*. After the glacier melted, the valley was drowned as the sea level rose. Spectacular fiords are found in Norway (page 30), New Zealand and southern Chile.
Fodder Crops Crops grown as food for animals.
Fold Mountains Mountains formed by folding layers of rocks. When parts of the Earth's *crust* move together from each side, the rocks in between are folded. The Andes are an example of a fold mountain range (page 154)
Geyser (Geysir) A hot spring which throws out a jet of hot water regularly or occasionally. Geysers occur in volcanic areas where water underground is heated so much that

▲ **A glacier** in the Swiss Alps, with stripes of moraine.

it turns to steam. The best-known geysers are in the USA, Iceland and New Zealand.

Glacier A mass of ice which moves slowly downhill. It follows the easiest route – usually along a river valley which it deepens and straightens. If the *climate* gets warmer, the glacier will gradually melt (see page 177).

Hurricane A severe tropical storm with spiralling winds of up to 340 km per hour and very low air pressure. The wind does a great deal of damage, and accompanying rain and high tides cause floods. The term is mainly used for Atlantic storms, which cause much damage in the USA, Central America and the West Indies. In the Pacific the same kind of storm is called a typhoon; in the Indian Ocean it is called a cyclone.

Hydro-Electric Power Electric power which is generated from a force of water passing through turbines in a power station. The force of water may be from a natural waterfall as at Niagara Falls, or it may be man-made by a dam or a pipeline.

Ice Ages Periods in the Earth's history when *ice sheets* have spread over large areas of the world which now have a much warmer climate. Between 700,000 and 10,000 years ago there were at least four Ice Ages in Europe and North America.

Ice Sheets A vast, thick area of ice which is slowly moving outwards under its own weight as new snow is added. The largest today covers Antarctica. In the Ice Ages, ice sheets covered much of Europe and North America. The moving ice scrapes the land (for example in Finland and north-east Canada). Melting ice sheets leave huge deposits of sands, gravels and *moraine*.

International Date Line An imaginary line near *longitude* 180° (see page 160).

Irrigation Watering the land to help grow crops. In many irrigation schemes, channels lead from a lake or river to the edge of fields. Gaps can be opened in these channels to let water flow on to each field when it is needed.

▲ **Irrigation water** is led from the dam in the background along mud channels to the crop.

Latitude and **Longitude** These are lines drawn on a globe. Lines which run through the poles north to south are called lines of longitude. The

▲ **An oasis** where water beneath the valley floor allows date palms to grow.

Equator and lines parallel to it are lines of latitude (see page 24).

Mediterranean Climate Summers are hot and dry; winters are warm and wet. Such a climate is found around the Mediterranean Sea and also in central California, central Chile, near Cape Town (South Africa) and near Perth (Australia).

Midnight Sun Seen in Polar lands in summer. Look at the diagram on page 180. In June the North Pole is tilted towards the sun, and places within the Arctic Circle receive 24 hours of sunlight. The opposite happens in December.

Monsoon The word means season and usually refers to winds that bring an exceptionally wet season for part of the year. The most spectacular monsoon climates are in Asia (see page 97). In summer, the continent heats up and becomes an area of low pressure. Winds are drawn in from the sea, bringing rain. In winter, the continent is cold with high pressure, and winds blow out from the land towards the ocean.

Moraine Loose rocks, gravel and clay carried by *glaciers* and *ice sheets*. Moraine is found on, in and under glaciers and ice sheets, and when they melt this material is dumped on the ground. Areas of moraine often have poor soil and poor drainage, giving marshy areas, such as in northern Poland.

Oasis An area in a *desert* with water at or near the surface. Crops can be grown, and people can live there, obtaining water from springs or wells.

Peninsula An area of land almost surrounded by water, but not completely cut off from the mainland. A good example is the Malay Peninsula (see page 86).

Plain A lowland area with a fairly level surface, though there may be hills. The North European Plain and the Great Plains of North America are examples of very large plains.

Plantation A large farm or estate on which only one *cash crop* is usually grown. Sometimes the first stages of processing take place there, such as drying the beans on a coffee plantation, or drying and crushing the leaves on a tea plantation.

Plateau An upland area with a

fairly level surface, though a plateau may have some hills and may be divided by deep valleys. Much of Eastern and Southern Africa is a plateau.

Polder An area of land reclaimed from a lake or the sea (see page 37).

Porous Rocks Rocks which allow water to sink through, for example chalk and sandstone. Water can often be collected from such rocks by wells or pumps.

Precipitation When used of the weather, refers to rain and snow.

Rain Forest Tropical forest in hot rainy or *monsoon* areas.

Relief A term used by geographers to mean the shape of the land. Mountains, valleys, plains, plateaus and depressions may give an area its shape. Relief maps indicate the shape of the land by colouring and shading, as in this atlas, or by contour lines which join up places with the same height.

Rift Valley A valley formed by movements of the earth. A block of land sinks down between deep faults in the Earth's *crust*. The largest is the Great Rift Valley, part of which is in East Africa (page 119). There are many other rift valleys: the River Rhine flows through one between Basle and Mainz.

▲ **Tundra landscape** in northern Norway.

Savanna Tropical grassland where it is hot all through the year. There are two seasons, a wet and a dry. The tall savanna grass is lush and green in the wet season, but brown and dry in the dry season. The scattered trees are the kind that can survive a long, hot drought, such as the baobab and acacia (see page 118).

Seasons Times of the year with distinct weather. People in *temperate lands* talk about hot and cold seasons (summer and winter); people in many tropical areas talk about wet

▼ **The Earth's** yearly path around the Sun.

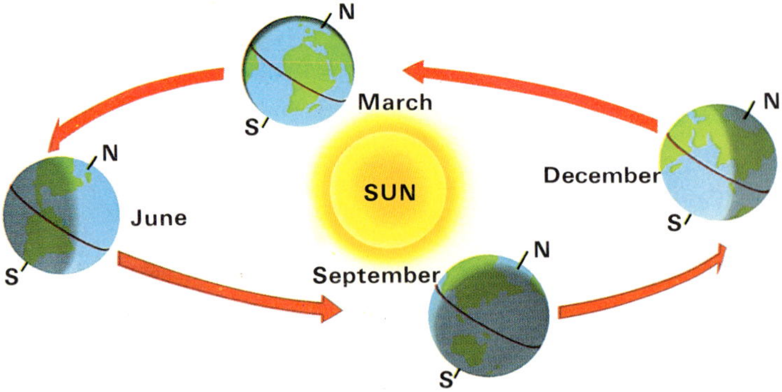

▲ **Light soil** is eroded by the wind in eastern England.

and dry seasons. Seasons occur because the Earth's *axis* is tilted. As the diagram below shows, in June the northern hemisphere tilts towards the Sun and receives greater heat and more daylight. In December, the southern hemisphere is tilted towards the Sun.

Sedimentary Rocks Rocks formed from sediments which once accumulated on land or sea. Most built up layer by layer under water and were gradually squeezed and cemented into layers of rocks. Clay, sandstone and limestone are examples of sedimentary rocks.

Soil Erosion The removal of valuable top soil. It is usually caused by bad farming methods. If large areas of soil are left bare, they may be washed away by heavy rain, and light soils may be blown away by strong winds. Some solutions are to *terrace* hillsides; to plant belts of trees to shelter fields; to plough along a slope instead of up and down it; to move animals before they eat all the grass and other plants.

Subsistence Farming Growing crops and/or keeping animals for the family's own needs. There will be little, if any, surplus to sell to others.

Temperate Lands Those parts of the world between the *Tropics* and the Polar areas which have a cold season and a hot season. Places such as the Mediterranean which have warm winters may be called warm temperate (see page 54). Places with cool winters may be called cool temperate (see page 31). Places with cold winters may be called cold temperate because they still have warm summers (see page 71).

Terraces Broad steps cut into the hillside to increase the amount of flat land for farming. Rice needs level land that can be flooded to exactly the same depth for the crop to grow well (see page 91). Terraces also help to prevent *soil erosion*.

Tropics Lines of *latitude* marking where the sun is directly overhead on midsummer's day. On June 21st, the sun is overhead at the Tropic of Cancer. On December 21st, it is overhead at the Tropic of Capricorn. Between these tropics are the tropical lands which are hot all year. Everywhere in the tropics, the sun is overhead at noon twice a year.

Tundra A treeless zone around the Arctic Circle where lichens and small plants grow in the short summers.

Wadi A dry watercourse in a *desert*. After a storm it may suddenly be filled with water.

Map Index

Index

Numbers in italics refer to illustrations.

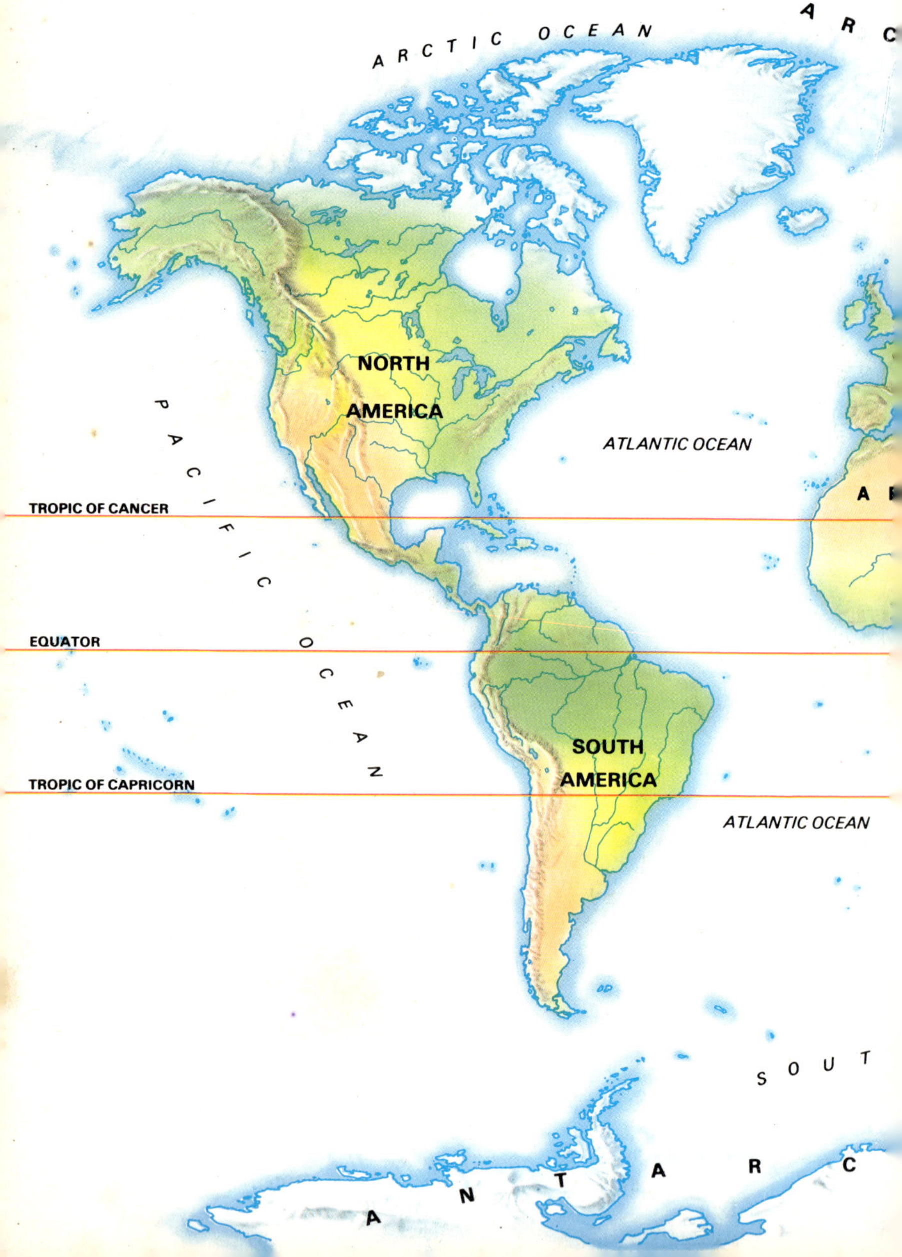
ARCTIC OCEAN
ARC
NORTH AMERICA
PACIFIC OCEAN
ATLANTIC OCEAN
A
TROPIC OF CANCER
EQUATOR
TROPIC OF CAPRICORN
SOUTH AMERICA
ATLANTIC OCEAN
SOUT
ANTARC